自由花がもっと楽しくなる本

池坊専永 監修

野田 学 著
Manabu Noda

JOY OF IKENOBO
FREE STYLE

『自由花がもっと楽しくなる本』によせて

華道家元四十五世　池坊専永

　野田学教授は英語を得意とされ、その能力を生かして大いに活躍していただいています。池坊中央研修学院では自由花研究室を担当し、そのアイデアに富んだ作品は、見る人の心をつかみます。

　自由花は、生活様式の変化に合わせて進化する花型です。その変化への対応方法もさまざまで、豊かな想像力が必要となります。

　想像力は、多くの物事を見て、知って、考えることで養われます。花のことだけでなく、多岐にわたるジャンルに興味を持つことで、作品の表現に生かすことができます。まさしく、想像力は創造力につながるのです。

　このたび刊行される『自由花がもっと楽しくなる本』は、こうした想像（発想）を作品へと創造していくプロセスがわかりやすく解説されています。自由花は、自由であるが故に何から手を付けていいのかわからなくなることがありますが、そうした不安や迷いを取り除き、自由花をより楽しむための一冊です。

　本書の刊行を機に、野田教授のさらなる飛躍に期待します。

はじめに

　長い歴史と伝統を持つ池坊いけばなは、日本人の暮らしの中で生まれ、育まれてきました。最古の花伝書といわれる『花王以来の花伝書』に記された作品群からは、室町時代の人々が花に思いを託し、暮らしの中に飾った様子が見られます。その後、武家社会や宮中で飾られたいけばなは、やがて立花へと発展します。一方で江戸時代中期以降、床の間に飾られるいけばなとして生花が生まれました。しかし、時が移り変わった現代の住環境においては、その床の間の減少が顕著です。

　「生活の移り変わりに従って、生き続け変わり続けているのが、いけばなの姿である」と池坊専永家元は述べられており、池坊専好次期家元も「生活文化は一部の人のみが享受するのではなく、より幅広い層がまさに生活の中で楽しんでこそ成り立つことができます」とおっしゃっています。

　本書では、お二人のこのお言葉を念頭に、池坊の伝統の心を現代に生かす今日の暮らしに適応した自由花への私見を述べさせていただき、その作例と手法などを掲載しています。また、世界へ広がる池坊として英語の対訳を付記しました。

　この本が、日々の暮らしの中で花とのふれあいを楽しむきっかけとなり、池坊自由花の世界を広げる一助となれば幸いです。

野田　学

Introduction

Ikenobo Ikebana, recognized through its long history and tradition, has been nurtured and cherished in Japanese life since its founding. From a series of works depicted in "*Kao Irai no Kadensho*" the oldest *kadensho,* we can imagine how people living in the Muromachi period used flowers to convey their thoughts and feelings and made displays of flowers as part of their daily lives. Ikebana was enjoyed in *samurai* society or at Court, and a style known as *rikka*, a work displayed in a larger space was typical in the houses of the well-to-do at that time. Further, in the middle and late Edo period, a space reserved for *tokonoma* became popular in Japanese architecture, where *shoka*, a style harmonizing with *tokonoma* was created. Now in the contemporary world, however, with the passing of each year, *tokonoma* is falling more and more out of favor.

Significantly, the Headmaster Sen'ei Ikenobo says "Ikebana shows a morphing style that prevails by changing as our lives change." The Headmaster Designate of Ikenobo, Senko Ikenobo also says, "Culture in our lifestyle is not something given to a limited number of people; it is something that becomes ubiquitous only when many different people from various walks of life can freely enjoy it."

With such valuable attitudes in mind, this handbook gives my perspective on free style, called *jiyuka* in Ikenobo, approach as a measure which brings the traditional Ikenobo spirit into modern times, including technical examples and methods.

Also for our global readers of Ikenobo, English translation is attached too.

I truly hope this book will be a strong motivator for you to enjoy your communication with flowers in daily life, and so helping enhance the world of Ikenobo *jiyuka*.

Manabu Noda

作品 1　うらじろ　椿　かすみ草　　**Work 1**　Materials: Gleichenia, Camellia, Gypsophila

もくじ
Contents

- 第一章　伝統の心を現代へ ……… 9
- 第二章　ドラマを創ろう ……… 24
- 第三章　自由花の楽しみ方 ……… 77
- 第四章　花と暮らそう！ ……… 101

- Chapter 1　Bringing the Traditional Spirit to the Present ……… 12
- Chapter 2　Making a Drama ……… 24
- Chapter 3　How to Enjoy *Jiyuka* ……… 78
- Chapter 4　Living with Flowers ……… 101

第一章 伝統の心を現代へ

池坊いけばなの伝統と時代性

　池坊550年祭の年であった2012年、池坊専永家元が「形から姿へ」というお言葉を発信されました。実は、これは1997年にも発信されています。「〜から〜へ」とは、移り変わりを意味しており、当代池坊の目指す方向性を示すもので、「理想的、あるいは美しい形を造る時代から、十人十色の草木の姿をいかす時代へ」ということだと認識しています。いけばなのいけ方や様式は時代とともに変化・発展するものですが、池坊の伝統の心は常に継承されるべきものです。

　専永家元が新風体を発表された際、「池坊の伝統的美感と構造を基本としながら、現代の諸事情に適応したものが新風体である」と定義付けられました。そこでこの章では、「池坊いけばなの伝統的美感と構造」と「現代における方向性」について考察します。

池坊いけばなの伝統的美感

　池坊いけばなの伝統的美感は、『池坊専応口伝』(『大巻』)に記された「草木の風興」、「おのつからおふる姿」と「宜しき面影」にあると考えられます。これらについて専永家元は「草木から得られる感情を素直に捉え、作為的でないことを池坊いけばなの基本としているのです」と述べられています。

　「風興」の「風」は「空気の動き」であり、それは目に見えない変化です。また、いけばなを構成する生きた植物の命というのも「常に変化していくもの」です。従って「風興」は、「刻々と変化する命あるものの趣」といえるのではないでしょうか。「おのつからおふる姿」とは草木が生育する出生と自然。言い換えれば、生まれと育ちに備わる個々の草木の姿の美しさだと考えます。そして、「宜しき面影」とは、草木美に対する着眼点と捉えることができます。

　ここで、「草木の風興」や「おのつからおふる姿」に基づく「宜しき面影」には、二面性があると考えられます。一つは出生美というおのおのの草木が生まれ持った個々の「らしさ」であり、例えば「梅は梅らしく」という美感です。もう一つは自然美という生育の過程において備わった一本一本の枝ぶりなどの個性です。いけばなの歴史を振り返ると、「松は松らしく」というような理想的な出生美に重点を置いた時代(明治期を中心とした時代など)と、十人十色の自然美に重点を置いた時代(二代専好が活躍した江戸初期など)があるようです。

　そして今、「形から姿へ」という方向性を持つ現代は、自然美を重視する時代であると考えられます。新風体が決められた形式を持たないということも、個々の草木の自然美を素直に生かすためだと思われます。

専正の老松除真立花図
Oimatsu Nokijin Rikka by Sensho

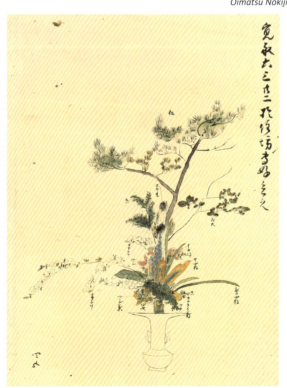

二代専好の老松除真立花図（真の枝ぶりが異なる二作）
Oimatsu Nokijin Rikka by Senko Ikenobo Ⅱ (Two works with different "*shin*" branches)

このような時代において、現代の池坊自由花についても、新風体と同じく自然美に着目して作者が思いを託すものであると考えます。ただし、自然美とは、自然にあるがままだけを意味するものではありません。『テキスト 池坊 立花―新風体』の序文にも「外界の景色としての自然ではなく、『おのずから溢れ出るもの』という意味である。……素材のもつ性質、特徴は、引き出し、見つけだすものである」と記されています。この点、池坊自由花においては自然美に対して自然な姿の全体的な美しさを捉える場合もあれば、自然が創り出した個々の草木が持つ色、形、質の美しさや部分の美的要素、いわゆる意匠美を表現に応じて生かす場合もあります。

いずれにしても命ある草木を見つめて、目には見えない趣をも含めたさまざまな美しさを生かすことが、池坊いけばなの伝統的美感であるといえます。

ここでもう一つ大切なことは、「いける」ということです。

専永家元は「挿すのではなく、いけなければなりません」「花を使った工作ならば、いけばなとは言えません」と述べられています。かつて、自由花といえば造形芸術志向が強い様式であったといえますが、これからの自由花においては作為的に作り過ぎず、草木の美しさを「いける」心を大切にしなければならないのだと思います。「いける」という言葉は、命あるものの「生きる」美しさと、自然が作り出した美しさを作品の中で「活かす（活用する）」ということを意味するものだと考えます。

花材を自由に用いることが許された自由花においても、池坊いけばなの伝統的美感を基として、草木から感じる美しさを素直に捉えなければなりません。「いける」ということを大切にしながら、作品を通して思いを表現することが、今後の自由花の基本だと思います。

池坊いけばなの伝統的構造

立花、生花、自由花のすべての様式において、池坊いけばなの根本理念である「和の精神」に基づく素材の取り合わせと構成が重要です。聖徳太子が説いた「和の精神」とは、「他を生かして共に生きる」という異なるものが互いに助け合い、高め合いながら生み出す調和の美です。立花や生花の「右長左短」「陰陽二体」などの教えにも、異なるもの同士による調和の美が感じられます。例えば「しだれ柳の真には、松やひのきの副が良い」という立花の教えも、葉のないものと常緑を取り合せた調和の美を意味するものです。つまり、対照と補完による調和の美的構成が池坊いけばなの伝統的構造となるのです。

● "まとめる"と"際立てる"：立花、生花に学ぶ

作品構成においては、程よい統一（まとめる）と変化（際立てる）が必要となります。いわゆる均衡と対照の美しさです。これらについて、立花や生花からも多くのことが学べます。

例えば、立花正風体の二カ所遣いや三カ所遣いが、"まとめる"テクニックの一例です。左右

に同じ花材を配することによって、作品にまとまりが生まれます。一方、主役となる花材を際立たせるために、あえて一カ所遣いとすることもあります。これが"際立てる"テクニックの一つです。これらのテクニックは、決められた形式を持たず花材を自由に扱える自由花においても活用すべき教えです。その他にも、立花正風体の構成法から自由花に活用できるものが多々あり、伝統ある立花の教えを自由花に生かすことは、単なる「自由ないけばな」ではなく、「池坊の伝統に基づく自由花」であるために大切であると考えます。

また、「引き算のいけばな」とも呼ばれる生花からは、省略による美の強調を学ぶことができます。草木を自然のまま器に挿すのではなく、草木に潜む美しさを引き出すための省略が"際立てる"テクニックの一つです。ミニチュアの作品は他のいけばな流派やフラワーデザインの世界にも存在しますが、池坊のミニチュア自由花の原点は、「省略の極み」と呼ばれる「椿一輪生」の考えであるといわれています。

Chapter 1 Bringing the Traditional Spirit to the Present
The tradition of Ikenobo Ikebana and its succession

In 2012, celebrating the 550th year of Ikenobo, the Headmaster Sen'ei Ikenobo expressed his idea in the words, "From Shape to Style." Here, Style refers to the natural or individual appearance of a plant. This remark has been expressed before too, back in 1997. The words "From to" in the expression show a change, which indicates the Ikenobo trend of the current Headmaster. I understand this as "From the period of ideal or beautiful shapes of flowers to the period of the uniqueness and individuality that each flower has." Simply because the method or style of ikebana can change or evolve as the time varies, the spirit of the Ikenobo tradition is perpetually handed down.

When the Headmaster Sen'ei Ikenobo introduced *shimputai*, it was defined as "a style accommodated to a modern setting based on the traditional beauty and structure of Ikenobo." In this chapter, let us consider "traditional sense of beauty and structure of Ikenobo" as well as "trends in modern times."

Traditional Sense of Beauty of Ikenobo Ikebana

The traditional sense of beauty of Ikenobo Ikebana is well expressed by three key words appearing in "*Ikenobo Senno Kuden*," the bible of Japanese ikebana: "*Somoku-no-fukyo*" (the inner character of living plants), "*Onozukara ouru sugata*" (the natural appearance of plants), and "*Yoroshiki omokage*" (beauty of the original impression given to us by each plant). For such key words, the Headmaster Sen'ei Ikenobo says, "the core basis of Ikenobo Ikebana should be a natural acceptance of feelings evoked by plants, and never be intentional."

The Chinese character of "*Fu*" in the Japanese word "*fukyo*," another meaning is "wind," means "the movement of air," which is something invisible. On the other hand, the life of living plants comprising Ikebana is also something always varying. "*fukyo*" (literally "atmosphere" or "taste") can be regarded as the intangible aspects of ever-changing life. The second key word, "*Onozukara ouru sugata*" is the beauty of nature, the beauty with which an individual plant is adorned at its birth and in its growing environment. The last key word, "*Yoroshiki omokage*" is the perspective on such beauty of plants.

Moreover, the word *"Yoroshiki omokage"* based on the concept of *"Somoku-no-fukyo"* or *"Onozukara ouru sugata"* has two sides to its meaning: one is the inherent nature of each plant as a plant type, as we often say, "Plum is beautiful as plum." The other is the individuality of each single tree or flower, acquired along with its growing environment. Looking back at ikebana history, these two different interpretations appeared separately; the former, the ideal natural beauty was evaluated mainly in Meiji period, and the latter, the beauty endorsed by individuality was more appreciated in the first Edo period (at which time Senko Ikenobo Ⅱ played a major role).

Now, in the contemporary world "From shape to style" is, I believe, the age which puts emphasis on individual natural beauty. This is well explained in *shimputai*, which has no specific form type, which leads to us how we can accept and enhance the individual natural beauty of each plant.

In contemporary Ikenobo *jiyuka* too, creators let the floral materials express their feelings or thoughts from the perspective of natural beauty, just as is so with *shimputai*. The natural beauty is, however, not the state as it is naturally found. In the introduction of "Textbook *rikka-simputai*," this natural beauty is described as follows: "This does not mean mere nature as external world scenery as occurring naturally, but the existence which spontaneously outpours. We have to draw out and find the nature or character of floral materials on our own." In Ikenobo *jiyuka*, sometimes we evaluate entire beauty of natural style, but at other times we enhance the beauty of various aspects such as color, shape, or texture of each individual branch or leaf or the beauty of a component, the designing beauty, in our expression.

Either way, the traditional beauty sense of Ikenobo dwells on the trial of expressing, reviving the variety of appeals of living plants, including invisible spiritual aestheticism.

Another crucial point here is *"ikeru,"* the core action for ikebana.

The Headmaster Sen'ei repeatedly remarked, "Don't put the flowers in vases; *revive* them," or "We do not use the term *ikebana* for just an artistic work that uses flowers." In the past, *jiyuka* was regarded as a style of art and design, but currently and in the future, we all should keep in mind how we can "revive" the beauty of plants, instead of excessive focus on artificial creativity. The Japanese word *"ikeru"* should mean both the beauty of "living" life and to "enhance" such natural beauty in our works.

Even in *jiyuka*, where floral materials can be used at one's discretion, we are not free from accepting and expressing the natural beauty we feel from plants based on the already stated traditional beauty sense of Ikenobo. More than anything, *"ikeru"* should be on our minds as a means to express ourselves through our works. I believe this is the basis of *jiyuka* from now on.

Traditional Structure of Ikenobo

In all the styles of *rikka*, *shoka*, and *jiyuka*, the combination and structure should be based on "the spirit of harmony" which is the principle of Ikenobo Ikebana. The spirit of harmony preached by Shotoku Taishi is the beauty of harmonization, such as "co-exist by respecting others," brought about by the collaboration and friendly competition of the different parties. In the model example of "*Ucho-Satan*" (Long in the right, short in the left) or "*In Yo Ni-tai*" (Double shapes of Yin, Yang), too, the beauty of harmony consists of different components. The rule in *rikka*, "for *Shin* of weeping willow, *Soe* of pine or Japanese cypress match" also mean the harmonization of leafless materials and ever-greens. Thus we can see that the aesthetic composition of harmony in contrast to complementation is Ikenobo's traditional structure.

●"Organize" *(Matomeru)* and "Emphasize" *(Kiwadateru)*: Learn from *Rikka* and *Shoka*

In the work structure, appropriate organization (*matomeru*) and emphasis (*kiwadateru*) is required. This is the so-called beauty of balance and comparison. For this, we can learn much also from *rikka* and *shoka*.

For example, "two-position" or "three-position" in *rikka shofutai* are a good examples of a organizing technique. By arranging the same floral materials on the right and left sides, a consistent, organized mood is generated in the work. On the other hand, to emphasize the main flower component, sometimes the material is positioned in one place only. This is one of the technique of "emphasizing (*kiwadateru*)." Such techniques are also the ones to apply in *jiyuka* that freely considers the floral materials without the setup format. We can learn many more from the structure method of *rikka shofutai* to reflect in *jiyuka*. Thus applying the traditional *rikka* teachings to *jiyuka* is meaningful when the it is not a mere "free ikebana" but "A Free Style based on the Ikenobo tradition."

The *shoka*, "often called Ikebana of subtraction," teaches us how to emphasize the beauty by minimization. Not using the flowers as they are, but using them in a minimal way is one of the techniques of minimization to draw out a true beauty from within the plants. There are miniature works also in other ikebana schools or in western floral designs, but the origin of Ikenobo miniature *jiyuka* are said to be *Tsubaki-Ichirin-ike*, "a single camellia" which is "the extreme case of minimization."

● 立花に学ぶ構成法

● Structure Method from *Rikka*

中心にラッパ水仙をいけ、存在感を高めると同時に、こでまりのなびきを強調するために片側にだけなびかせます。さらに作品にまとまりを与えるために、しゃがを左右に配しました。立花の二カ所遣いによる統一感と一カ所遣いによる強調の応用です。

The daffodil in the center to increase the presence, and slant the meadowsweet branch to only a single side to emphasize its gentleness. To make the entire work balance, position two seedlings of fringed iris on the right and left sides. An application of organizing measure using "two-position" and emphasizing measure with "single-position" used in *rikka*.

こでまり　ラッパ水仙　しゃが　鳴子ゆり　都忘れ
Materials: Spiraea cantoniensis (meadowsweet), Daffodil, Iris japonica (fringed iris), Solomon's seal, Miyamayomena savatieri

作品2　こでまり　ラッパ水仙　しゃが　鳴子ゆり　都忘れ
Work 2　Materials: Spiraea cantoniensis (meadowsweet), Daffodil, Iris japonica (fringed iris), Solomon's seal, Miyamayomena savatieri

立花の正真は、後囲とともに立てる様式を強調するものですが、同時に前後左右に広がる他の部分を際立たせる働きもあります。作品では、垂直に用いたクロトンの葉が空間を引き締めながら、全体の左右への広がりを際立たせています。

Shoshin of *rikka* emphasizes the vertical style along with *ushirogakoi*, but at the same time this helps emphasize the other parts extending front, rear, right, and left. In the work, the leaves of croton arranged vertically pepper the atmosphere, and emphasize the entire stretch to the lateral orientation.

BEFORE

バンダ　ななかまど　パープル・ファウンテングラス　ヒペリクム
Materials: Vanda orchid, Mountain ash, Pennisetum, Hypericum

AFTER

作品3　バンダ　ななかまど　パープル・ファウンテングラス　ヒペリクム　クロトン
Work 3　Materials: Vanda orchid, Mountain ash, Pennisetum, Hypericum, Croton

BEFORE

AFTER

縞ふとい　スネークアリウム　コチョウラン　紫ラン
Materials: Scirpus tabernaemontani 'Zebrinus', Allium, Phalaenopsis aphrodite orchid, Bletilla striata orchid

作品 4　縞ふとい　スネークアリウム
コチョウラン　紫ラン　鳴子ゆり
Work 4　Materials: Scirpus tabernaemontani 'Zebrinus', Allium, Phalaenopsis aphrodite orchid, Bletilla striata orchid, Solomon's seal

直線と曲線の対比を狙った作品で、花器口を1輪のコチョウランで引き締めています。引き締めるだけでは窮屈な印象を与えるため、鳴子ゆりの緑葉の広がりをコチョウランの左右に配することで、少し緩める働きを持たせます。これは、立花の前置と留の働きの関係に似た構成法です。

It is a work to enjoy contrast between the lines and curves, with a single phalaenopsis aphrodite orchid accentuated at the vase inlet. The orchid can tighten the entire mood, but to balance it, the green leaves of Solomon's seal are positioned around the orchid, for a slightly more relaxed impression. This uses a structure method similar to the roles of *maeoki* and *tome* in *rikka*.

えのころ草のなびく美しさを捉えて放射状に構成しましたが、器の重量感に対して弱く散漫に見えます。そこで、面的なカラテアの葉を加えて背景とすることで主役の動きを補うとともに、空間を引き締めました。カラテアは、役枝の枝物の空間を引き締める立花の大葉と同様の働きをしています。

To express the beauty of bowing foxtail grass, the seedlings are structured radially. Still, they look fragile and scattered compared to the imposing feeling of the vessel. Then, the broad leaves of calathea are positioned in the background, to support the movement of main foxtail grass as well as to pepper the atmosphere. Here, calathea works just as "*oha*" (large leaves) in *rikka* to pepper the atmosphere of main branches.

BEFORE

えのころ草　ききょう　ほととぎす　ヘリコニア
Materials: Foxtail grass, Japanese bellflower, Japanese toad lily, Heliconia

AFTER

作品5　えのころ草　ききょう　ほととぎす　ヘリコニア　カラテア
Work 5　Materials: Foxtail grass, Japanese bellflower, Japanese toad lily, Heliconia, Calathea

大きく開いたてっせんの軽やかで印象的な美しさを捉えた掛け花です。てっせんに動感を与えるために、矢筈すすきの葉1枚と小判草1本を添えました。立花の『習物七ヶ条』の一つである「薄一葉」の応用です。

This is a hanging arrangement that catches the light and charming beauty of the blooming clematis. To add dynamism to clematis, a leaf of eulalia and a seedling of quaking grass are added. This is an application of "*Susuki hito-ha*," one of "*Naraimono Nanakajo*" (Seven Studies) of *rikka*.

BEFORE

てっせん　レクス・ベゴニア　るり玉あざみ　サンダーソニア
Materials: Clematis, Begonia, Globe thistle, Sandersonia

AFTER

作品 6　てっせん　矢筈すすき　小判草　レクス・ベゴニア　るり玉あざみ　サンダーソニア
Work 6　Materials: Clematis, Eulalia, Briza maxima (quaking grass), Begonia, Globe thistle, Sandersonia

● 生花に学ぶ：省略の美

　池坊のミニチュア自由花は、花材のごく細かな部分まで観察して美を見いだすことから始まります。それが、生花の「椿一輪生」を原点とする「省略の美」といわれるゆえんです。自然が作り出した花の表情や大小、わずかな茎の曲がりや葉のひねりなど、花材の持つ美的要素を見極めながら必要な部分を抜き出して作品に生かします。

● Learn from Shoka: Minimized beauty

A miniature *jiyuka* in Ikenobo starts from finding beauty by observing the individual materials in detail. This is why Ikenobo works are appraised as "Minimized beauty" typically represented by the single camellia *shoka* called "*Tsubaki-Ichirin-ike*." The impression of flowers or the size of them, a slight bending of stems or warping of leaves, all of which occur naturally—such aesthetic elements of materials are elaborately identified to be extracted and represented in a work.

作品 7　じゅずさんご
小菊　ヒューケラ

Work 7　Materials: Rivina humilis, Small chrysanthemum, Heuchera

作品 8　バラ　オブリザツム　ラビットファン
Work 8　Materials: Rose, Obryzatum orchid, Davallia fejeensis

1本のバラの美しいと感じた部分を切り取って主役としました。さらに黄色い小花を取り合わせることで、バラの花を大きく見せています。小さな作品の中にも大小の変化を考えることが大切です。

The part of a rose, which impressed me with its beauty, is taken to be the main character of the work. Further, combining it with yellow small flowers emphasizes the large comparative size of the rose. It is important to give a contrast in size even in a small work.

作品 9　アルストロメリア　ぼけ　玉しだ　しらが松　ブルーキャッツアイ
Work 9　Materials: Alstroemeria, Japanese quince, Sword fern, Variegated pine, Otacanthus caeruleus

ぼけの枝で作った空間に、1輪のアルストロメリアを主役とし、器から飛び出すようにいけました。その他の花材は、さまざまな役割（みずみずしさ、色彩の対照、前後のバランスなど）を持った脇役です。おのおの自由な取り合わせと構成には、それぞれの花材に果たすべき役割がなければなりません。

A space is created with Japanese quince, with an arrangement of a single alstroemeria so that it overflows out of the vase. Other materials each play a supporting role with their individuality (such as freshness, color contrast, and balance between front and rear). In a free combination and structure, they always need specific roles to be assigned.

作品 10 てっせん おみなえし 日々草
Work 10 Materials: Clematis, Patrinia scabiosifolia, Madagascar periwinkle

グリーティングカードの表紙に花入れを取り付けて舞台としました。まるでフクロウがかわいい1輪のてっせんを見つめているようです。花器以外の物も工夫によってはドラマの舞台として活用することができる一例です。

Mounting a bowl onto the greeting card cover received, I made a small stage for the flowers. An owl is staring at a lovely clematis flower. This shows many things other than the typical vase's work as a stage for a flowery drama as we attractively adjust them.

作品 11　パンジー　プテリス　レースフラワー　南天
Work 11　Materials: Pansy, Pteris, Lace flower, Nandina

香水瓶を器として、色違いのパンジーをひな祭りのお内裏さまとおひなさまのようにいけました。ワイヤーによって空間を限定するとともに、その先に南天の実を付けてリズム感を出しています。また、花器に近い色の敷物で統一感を与えました。

In two perfume bottles, a pair of pansies in different colors are sitting just like the emperor and the empress during *Hina-matsuri,* the Festival of Dolls. Each space is limited by a wire, and berries of nandina attached to the wire give a rhythm to the work. The cloth of a similar color to that of the vase pulls the whole look of the work together.

第二章 ドラマを創ろう

花は役者、器は舞台
ドラマの役者
　花材となる草木は、作者の表現に基づくドラマを演じる役者ともいえますが、草木美には二つの捉え方があります。一つは「花、葉、枝」という草木の自然的な捉え方であり、もう一つは「色、形、質」という個々の花材が持つ美的要素に着目する捉え方です。

● 花、葉、枝
・花：在来種の花には季節感が備わっています。例えば、桜の木は一年中生い立っていますが、その開花時期から「桜は春」というものです。このことから、同季の花材を取り合わせることによって季節感を表現できます。

Chapter 2 Making a Drama
Flower is a player, Vase is a stage
Cast of drama
The plants are in a way the cast of the drama written by the ikebana creator with his/her expression. There are two triggers of understanding the beauty of plants: one is "flower, leaf, and branch" which is a natural way of understanding, and the other is "color, shape, and texture" which is a way of focusing on the aesthetic element that individual floral material holds.

●Flowers, leaves, branches
・**Flowers:** Native flowers possess the sense of season. For example, the cherry tree stands all through the year, but we regard it as a sign of spring because of its flowers blooming. From this, combining the floral materials in the same season for example can express the season well.

秋の花を取り合わせて季情を表現しました。日本では秋桜とも呼ばれるコスモスとともに、「私も紅くてきれいなのよ！」という意味の名を持つわれもこう（吾亦紅）の主張を放射的な構成で取り合わせました。小菊の花と葉の用い方は、作品4（16ページ）と同様です。

The autumn scene is expressed by the combination of autumn flowers. The combination consists of cosmos, another name in Japan is "autumn cherry blossoms," and great burnet whose name means "Look at me, I am so pretty in red." in a radial structure. The use of flowers and the leaves of small chrysanthemum is the same as that in Work 4 (page: 16).

Work 4: refer to page 16 参照 ▶ P16 作品 4

作品 12　コスモス　われもこう　小菊
Work 12　Materials: Cosmos, Great burnet, Small chrysanthemum

- 葉：「緑は命の色」といわれますが、それは、季節の移り変わりとともに葉の様子が変化していく中で、緑の時が一番生き生きとしているからです。春の若葉が夏には緑葉になり、秋には先枯れしたり紅葉したりします。そして、冬には落葉するのが一般的な葉の移り変わりです。

  紅葉には紅葉の、枯葉には枯葉のよさがありますが、活力みなぎるのはやはり緑の葉の時でしょう。松や万年青（おもと）が祝儀の花材とされるのは、いつも青々とした常緑だからです。「松のようにいつも青々と元気で！」という思いに、日本の伝統的な感情表現が見られる一例です。

  生花の二種生に「花のないものに花を添えて」という教えがありますが、「葉のないものに葉を添えて」という二種生はありません。これは、まず葉があって生きる命の美しさを感じるということです。きれいに咲いた花だけでなく葉が大切であり、命の営みを感じる葉を重要視するのが池坊いけばなの美感なのです。

  例えば、秋に美しい花を咲かせる彼岸花がかつて禁花であった理由は、火を思わせると同時に、葉を伴わずに咲く花でもあったからといわれています。しかし、現代の外来種や園芸種では、葉のない花茎だけで販売されているものが数多くあります。生花三種生や生花新風体では、これらの花を用いて他の葉を取り合わせることが可能です。いわゆる時代に適応した知恵といえるでしょう。いずれにしても池坊いけばなにとっては、命を表現する葉が重要なのです。フリースタイルとも呼ばれる自由花の場合は、葉を用いずに作品を構成することも可能ですが、基本的には生命感のある緑を加えるべきだと考えます。

- **Leaves:** The color green is often used for an image of life. Because, as the leaves change according to the season, they are most fresh when they are green. The young small leaves in spring grow to green in summer, and change color or even fade in autumn. Then they finally drop in winter–that is the normal course of change that leaves follow.
  Even the colored leaves or fallen leaves are themselves beautiful, the vigor of the leaves can be best expressed in green. The reason why pine or Japanese rhodea are popular for celebrating occasions is because they are evergreen. It is a good example to show the Japanese traditional sense of beauty when pine is seen as a symbol of freshness and health.
  There is a rule in the "*Nishu-ike*" (work consisting of two types of materials) in *shoka*; "Add a flower to a flowerless scene." Yet there is no *Nishu-ike* to apply a rule, "Add a leaf to a scene containing no leaves." This means, to feel the beauty of something alive, a piece must contain green foliage in the first place. Not only beautifully blooming flowers, but also foliage is crucially evaluated in Ikenobo Ikebana, for the leaves take a more basic and direct role in the sustenance of life.
  For example, the reason why the cluster amaryllis (Lycoris radiate) that blooms beautifully in autumn was once prohibited in Ikenobo Ikebana, is because it is said that it reminds us of fire, and it is a flower without leaves. However, today we see many flower stems without leaves on the market, mainly exotic species or garden species. In "*Sanshu-ike*" (work consisting of three types of materials) in *shoka* or *shoka shimputai,* these flowers are used with other leafy materials. This is something like wisdom gained as the times change. In summary, Ikenobo Ikebana values the foliage as an expression of life force. *Jiyuka* can constitute a work even without leaves, but I generally believe we should add greenery to make our works lively and vivid.

作品 13　夏はぜ　ききょう　なでしこ
Work 13　Materials: Vaccinium oldhamii (Oldham blueberry), Japanese bellflower, Pink

夏はぜの緑葉の美しさを表現するために葉表を前に向けていけ、緑葉のエネルギー溢れるさまを捉えました。輪郭を整えながら、一部に葉のない枝を見せて空間にめりはりを付けています。「統一と変化」の一例です。

To express the beautiful Oldham blueberry, there is a framing of an energetic spread of green leaves, mainly facing toward the front. As the outline is nicely trimmed, a space created by a leafless branch helps to add a sophisticated air to the entire work. A good example of "organization and a variation."

・枝：枝や茎からは、草木の生きてきた様子が感じられます。茎がまっすぐな園芸種に対して「風情がない」というのは、紆余曲折を経た成長を感じないからでしょう。つまり、枝や茎によって草木が生きようとする動感などを表現することができるということです。

- **Branches:** We can feel how plants live from observing their branches or stems. If we feel that some look somewhat less attractive in the garden species with their stems just straight, it is because we tend to think their lives may be without twists or turns that we naturally encounter in our own lives.
  This is, in a way, a means that we can express the dynamism of life by using branches or stems.

作品 14　夏はぜ　あじさい　ききょう
Work 14　Materials: Vaccinium oldhamii (Oldham blueberry), Hydrangea, Japanese bellflower

前作では夏はぜの緑葉の美しさを捉えましたが、この作品では枝ぶりの風情を生かしています。枝の動きを見せるために思い切って葉を省略しました。同じ花材でも作者の思いによって用い方が変わります。「省略による強調」を意識した作例の一つです。

In the previous work the beauty of greenery was the focus, but this time the work concentrates on the handsome branches of Oldham blueberry. To show the movement of branches, leaves are daringly cut out in some parts. Even with the same materials, the way of using greatly depends on the creator and what the creator wants to express. This work, "emphasis through minimalism" is one example of which I am aware.

● 色、形、質

おのおのの草木は、独特の色、形、質を備えています。ここで重要なのは、これら三種が同時に備わっているということです。絵の具は色を備えており、作者が描くことで初めて形が与えられるものですが、草木には色も形も質も最初から備わっているのです。「絵画や彫刻は、無から有。いけばなは、有から有」という専永家元のお言葉が意味することの一つだといえます。

- 色：同じ赤い花でも、バラとチューリップ、あるいはゆりでは感じるものが全く異なります。形や質も考慮した上で表現に応じた色を選択しなければなりません。私見ですが、同じ紫の花でも日本のききょうには風がそよぐ「爽やかさ」を感じ、トルコぎきょうからは水に関連する「清らかさ」を感じます。これは、花びらの質感の相違によるものだといえます。

●Color, shape, and texture

Each plant possesses specific characteristics of color, shape, and texture. The important thing here is it is equipped with color, shape, and texture at the same time. Paint is the tool for adding color to a shape, where a shape only exists after the creator has drawn it. But living plants originally have both, as well as texture. This eloquently explains the meaning of the Headmaster Sen'ei Ikenobo's words, "Painting and sculpture bring something from nothing, but ikebana brings something from something."

- **Color:** Even with the same red color, roses and tulips, and lilies create totally different impressions to us. So we have to choose an appropriate color according to what we want to express, but considering shape and texture also. This is my personal impression, that the Japanese bellflower gives a freshness which for me evokes a cool breeze, while prairie gentian has a purity that reminds me of water. This all is for the difference of texture in the petals.

秋色の花材と器を取り合わせ、色彩と共に大小の丸い形のリズム感で錦秋を表現しました。ザラッとした質感のベゴニアの葉も季節感を高める脇役です。黄緑色のアレカヤシの葉の広がりで秋風を表しました。

Combining the materials of autumn-color, the colorful rich autumn is expressed with a repeating pattern of circular shapes, large and small, using the repeating color. The textured taste of begonia leaves also helps to improve the suggestion of the season's mood. Stretching of the palm leaves in yellow-green color express an autumn breeze in the work.

作品 15
ピンクッション
おみなえし
ゆうぎり草
レクス・ベゴニア
小菊　アレカヤシ

Work 15
Materials:
Pincushions,
Patrinia scabiosifolia,
Throatwort,
Begonia,
Small chrysanthemum, Palm

・**形**：形について「点」「線」「面」「マッス」という言葉がよく用いられますが、ここで注意しなければならないのは、「点」と「線」と「面」、さらには「マッス」を取り合わせさえすれば自由花作品が出来上がるわけではないということです。

例えば、単純に「点はひまわり、線はニューサイラン、面はモンステラ」というような取り合わせ方には、何の表現意図もありません。もちろん、上記の取り合わせが悪いわけではありませんが、ドラマを演じる役者には果たすべき役割があり、作品を構成する花材にも役割がないといけないのです。言い換えれば、草木の色や形や質に着目する自由花では、「表現に基づき、花材に果たすべき役割や意味を与える」ということが重要となります。

- **Shape:** When taking about shape, the key words "Point, line, surface, and mass" are popular. Here we need to be careful to eliminate a common misunderstanding that *jiyuka* is completed only when we can mix the elements of "Point line, surface, and mass." For example, depending on the typical mixture of "Sunflower for point, New Zealand Flax for line, and Monstera for surface" this has no meaningful expression. This combination itself is not so poor actually, but what I mean is that every material in a work should have a role to play, such as every player in a drama. In other words, in *jiyuka* which focuses on the color, shape, and texture of the plants, the point is "to give the materials the roles to play in a work based on the desired expression."

動物の顔のようにも見えるアンスリウムから発想し、花の形の寓意性を生かした作品です。花入れとアルミ線で胴体のような土台を作りました。主役の大きな花を際立たせるために小花を取り合わせ、手を広げたように配した玉しだでみずみずしさを添えています。

An expression inspired by the flower of anthurium which is shaped like an animal's face, and making full use of this symbolism in the flower shape. The base is made like the body of the animal, composed of a vase and aluminum wire. Small flowers play the role of highlighting the large flower, the main cast, and the sword fern arranged as the open hand adds freshness.

作品 16　アンスリウム　玉しだ　桜小町（シレネ）　ゴールデンスティック
Work 16　Materials: Anthurium, Sword fern, Silene, Craspedia globosa (Golden sticks)

- 質：日本のききょうとトルコぎきょうの質の相違につい前述しましたが、質というものは、頭の中でイメージするだけでは感じ取れないことが多々あります。作品の制作過程でしっくりこないときは、色や形は良くても質が他の花材や器と調和しない場合が多いものです。例えば、艶のあるガラス器に枝物をいけた時、花器の艶によってゴツゴツした質感を持つ木の枝が汚く見えることがあります。

- **Texture:** As in the former explanation on texture differences between the Japanese bellflower and Prairie gentian, texture is something that we cannot always grasp from imagination only. When we feel the work is unfit or unnatural, less harmonized in some way as it is being worked on, it may often be the case of the texture, in which the texture or density of the material does not match the other materials or the vases, even though its color or shape is perfect. For example, when we use materials with many branches in a glossy glass vessel, branches with a rugged texture can give a rough impression, which is not compatible with the tone of the glass vessel.

作品 17　梅　ラッパ水仙　葉ぼたん　シクラメン

Work 17　Materials: Japanese plum, Daffodil, Flowering cabbage, Cyclamen

土っぽい材質の水盤と苔むした梅の枝のつくる空間に柔らかな春の草花を配し、質感の対照美に季節の移り変わりを捉えました。苔木の間に見せた水面が水の清らかさを表現し、早春を演出する役割を担っています。

A clay basin and a mossy plum branch creates space, in which soft gentle spring flowers are placed to express the season change through the beauty of texture contrast. The purity of the water is evoked by allowing the water surface to be visible from between the mossy branches, so as to let the plants produce an early spring.

ドラマの舞台

　作品に用いる花器、あるいはレリーフやタペストリー、モビールなどの土台は、草木という役者がドラマを演じる舞台であるともいえます。生花では花材の出生や枝ぶりに合わせて花器を選ぶという教えがありますが、自由花では役者（花材）に合わせて舞台（花器）を選ぶこともあれば、舞台（花器）に合わせて役者（花材）を選ぶこともあります。後者の場合は、いわゆる「花器からの発想」です。自作の器（土台）やレリーフなどでは、土台を作成してから花材を選ぶことも多く、この場合も「花器からの発想」といえるでしょう。

　また、自作の土台（器やレリーフなど）を作成する場合は、制作意図や表現を設定しながら素材を選んで構成することも大切です。単なる「変わった造形」を試みるのではなく、表現に基づく土台作りをしなければなりません。自由花では、「器も表現の一部」といわれます。さらに、水盤などの広口の花器を用いたときは、花器の中に見える水や石なども表現のための素材ということになります。見えるものはすべて作品の一部であり、表現に基づくものであると考えるとき、花留などの工夫も必要になることが多々あります。また、器の下に敷く敷物も作品の一部となります。上記の事柄のさまざまな効果を考えながら、工夫していきましょう。

● 花器の原点と発展

　いにしえの時代には、現代のような花器業者は存在しなかったでしょう。いけばなが生まれて発展し始めた時代の絵図を見ると、中国などから渡来した祭器や生活雑器を用いて花をいける器としていたことがわかります。また、室町時代の『花王以来の花伝書』の中には、急須に花を挿して机の上に飾る机花や、おみくじを入れる筒を花器に活用した掛け花の絵図が掲載されています。

　そこから推察すると、現代における籠の花入れも、もともとは魚籠や野菜などを入れる籠だったのでしょう。つまり、今では立花や生花をいけるための格調高い花器と認識されているものも、その原点はいけばな用の花器ではなく、後に花器として発展し考案されたものが数多くあるのではないでしょうか。

　本書は、「伝統の心を現代へ」を基本的な方向性として、現代生活に適応する池坊自由花の紹介を主な目的の一つとしています。そこで、花展などに用いられる特別な花器や非日常的な花器ばかりではなく、誰もが持っているような花器に加えて生活雑器を花入れに活用した作品も多く掲載しています。

　前述のように、自由花ではドラマの舞台となるさまざまな色、形、質を持つ器に加えて、作者自身が草木美を生かすための舞台を制作することも可能です。「置く」「掛ける」「つる」という構成の中で飾る環境や表現に応じた創意工夫を施し、自由花の世界を広げましょう。

Stage for a drama

A vase is used for work, as well as the base materials such as reliefs, tapestries, or mobiles, and can be thought of as a stage for the cast of plants to play out a drama. According to the *shoka* rule, a vase must be selected according to the nature or shape of branches of materials. While in *jiyuka*, we sometimes choose a "stage" (vase) according to the "actors" (floral materials), or vice versa. When we choose the floral materials according to the vase, it means "impression taken from the vase" Especially, if we use a self-built vase (base) or relief, we often choose materials after completion of such a base, so this is also the case with "impression taken from the vase."

For the self-built/DIY base (vase or relief), it should be carefully structured by appropriate choices made for the base materials according to the configuration of the production image or intention. Instead of just depending on a mere "unique self-made" shaped form, think how the base matches what is imagined or the intention. *Jiyuka* evaluates a vase as, "one of the components of the expression." Further, when we use a basin with a wider opening, water or pebbles inside the basin are also materials to produce the whole desired expression. Anything present there is an element of the work based on the image and intention; this concept leads us to another effort by paying attention to a tool such as a *hanadome* (flower support). Of course, rags placed under the work are also one of the constituents. We need to consider various effects from using the above elements for further expression.

● Origin of the vase and its development

In early times, there would have been no vase vendors as we have now. The historical pictures drawn in the period when ikebana was founded and developed teach us that the holders originally used in religious ceremonies or in regular use in China or other countries were brought over to Japan and used as flower vases. Also, the "*Kao Irai no Kadensho*" from the Muromachi period includes drawings of flowers in a tea pot decorating a desk, or hanging arrangement using a box for *omikuji* (fortune-telling tickets) as a vase.

Judging from this, the design of flower basket we currently use for ikebana was originally a basket intended to contain fish or vegetables. Many elegant vases we now regard as sophisticated for *rikka* or *shoka* can be traced back to origins designed as tools for different purpose other than *ikebana*, and which were gradually developed and refined to be what we see now.

This book is mainly intended for introducing the Ikenobo *jiyuka* to match contemporary times based on the principle "conveying the traditional spirit to our modern times." This is why the book contains many works utilizing everyday items, such as bowls or basins, that anyone has for use as flower vases, in addition to elaborate, special vases which we can only see in artistic flower exhibitions.

As previously stated, *jiyuka* allows the creator to make a stage of a unique drama to reveal the beauty of plants and other materials. To pursue this purpose, the creator can even make a vase on his/her own, or select a vase from various choices of color, shape, and texture. I hope every creator develops in the world of *jiyuka* using an inventive, imaginative approach according to the environment or expression in the constituent options of "standing," "hanging," and "suspended" styles.

花王以来の花伝書：机花と籤筒花の絵図
"*Kao Irai no Kadensho*": Drawings of flowers on a desk and flowers in *omikuji* (fortune-telling tickets) box

● 水盤を舞台として

水盤を用いる作品は、水の見せ方について意識を向けることが大切です。単に花材を養うための水ではなく、表現の一部としての水の見せ方を考えましょう。そのためには、花留の工夫なども必要になる場合があります。

● Using a basin as a stage

When using a basin, it is important to be careful how we can show the water contained in it. Think of water as not only a substance for nurturing flowers, but as a crucial element of your expression. To do this, we also need to be conscious of how to use a *hanadome* (flower support).

参照 ▶ P72 作品 63
Work 63: refer to page 72

作品 18　スプレンゲリ　アンスリウム　レウココリネ　ヘリコニア
Work 18　Materials: Asparagus 'Splengeri', Anthurium, Leucocoryne, Heliconia

水盤の中に鏡面仕上げの塩ビ板を敷き、板を保護する水色のシートを部分的にカットして水面(みなも)のように見せたものを土台としています。若々しい緑に清らかな色と質感を持つ花を配して、春の水ぬるむ頃を表現しました。花留には吸盤を使用しています。

As a base, a mirror-finish PVC sheet is placed in the basin, and a light blue protective sheet is partially cut into a simulated water surface. With the help of bold touch, pure color of flowers organized with fresh greenery, the work expresses a spring season of warming water. Suction cups are used for a *hanadome* (flower support).

参照 ▶ P63 作品 54
Work 54: refer to page 63

作品 19　いたやかえで　トルコぎきょう　アネモネ
Work 19　Materials: Maple, Prairie gentian, Anemone

内側がブルーのグラデーションになっている器から発想し、緑が美しい初夏の湖畔を表現しました。器の外にいたやかえでの枝を伸ばして、山間に広がる新緑の美しさを感じさせます。作品では、いたやかえでの枝の"又"の部分を利用して草花を留めています。花留を工夫して水面をたっぷりと見せることがポイントです。

Inspired by a bowl which has blue gradation inside, I expressed a lakeside with beautiful green in early summer. The maple is stretched over the bowl, representing the beautiful green of the season over a mountain valley. In this work the two-forked part of the maple is used as a *hanadome* (flower support); an effective *hanadome* shows the water surface as much as possible and helps improve the impression of the work.

参照 ▶ P15 作品3
Work 3: refer to page 15

作品 20　睡蓮　けむり草　縞ふとい　日々草
Work 20　Materials: Water lily, Smoke tree, Scirpus tabernaemontani 'Zebrinus', Madagascar periwinkle

朝もやの中で睡蓮が美しい花を咲かせている情景を表現しています。けむり草で水盤を覆うように構成し、水面を見せながら睡蓮の美しさを捉えました。垂直に立てた縞ふといのシャープさがけむり草の柔らかな広がりを強調していますが、これは作品3（15ページ）と同様の構成法です。

The work expresses a scene in which a water lily blooms in the morning mist. Smoke tree is positioned to cover the basin, and a beautiful water lily is arranged with the visible water surface. The sharp impression of Zebrinus emphasizes the soft cluster of smoke tree, which uses the same structure as in Work 3 (page 15).

オブリザツムの黄色い小花で水面に輝く陽光を表現しています。紫色のレウココリネを取り合わせ、色彩の対照美とリズム感を求めました。バラの花葉で空間を引き締めながら、カラーの茎を細く切って波紋のように配することで水面を連想させています。花留は、半透明のプラスチック製ネットを筒状にしたものを使用しました。

The small yellow obryzatum orchid flowers express sunlight shining on the water surface. Combined with purple leucocoryne flowers, the contrast in color and the sense of rhythm are emphasized. The rose flower and the leaves placed in the middle add a sharp image to the space, and the calla stem, cut thin, evokes an image of ripples on the water surface. *Hanadome* (flower support) is a semi-transparent plastic, net patterned cylinder.

参照 ▶ P73 作品 64
Work 64: refer to page 73

作品 21　オブリザツム　レウココリネ　カラー　バラ
Work 21　Materials: Obryzatum orchid, Leucocoryne, Calla, Rose

蓮の葉に似た丸い葉と明るい彩りの花を咲かせるナスタチウムに「夏の水辺」への思いを映しました。挿し口を分割して構成することで、器の色合いも生かしています。また、メタリックなビーズを通したアルミ線を花留として、水面を美しく見せました。

Here we see the round leaves similar to those of the water lily and the bright colored flowers of nasturtium. These are the "cast" of the stage, "Summer Waterside." The organization of split positioning of the flowers makes the beautiful basin color fully visible. Also, the aluminum wire decorated with metallic beads is used as *hanadome* (flower support) to emphasize the beauty of the water surface.

参照 ▶ P65 作品 56
Work 56: refer to page 65

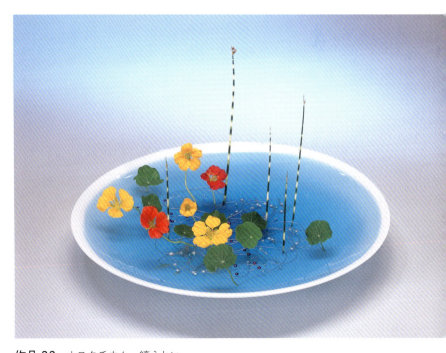

作品 22　ナスタチウム　縞ふとい
Work 22　Materials: Nasturtium, Scirpus tabernaemontani 'Zebrinus'

千代萩の涼感を生かすため、水盤にゆったりと配しました。縞ふといで伸びやかさを添え、紫と白と緑だけですっきりとまとめています。花留はペットボトルの底の部分を活用しました。

Each element is organized with ample space around it to express the cool feeling of Siberian lupin. Adding the growing energy of Zebrinus, the work is coordinated with minimal cool colors of purple, white, and green. For *hanadome* (flower support), the base part of PET bottles is used.

参照 ▶ P69 作品 60
Work 60: refer to page 69

作品 23　千代萩　縞ふとい
Work 23　Materials: Thermopsis lupinoides (Siberian lupin), Scirpus tabernaemontani 'Zebrinus'

冬の湖面にしんしんと降る雪をイメージしたかすみ草と、真っ赤な紅葉が移りゆく季節感を表現しています。情感の演出のために1輪のコスモスが水面に浮かぶように配しました。コスモスの花留には透明の吸盤を用いています。

Gypsophila, the image of snow falling on the winter lake, along with red leaves, expresses the changing season. To effectively produce the situation, a single cosmos is arranged so that it floats on the lake surface. A transparent suction cup is used for the *hanadome* (flower support) of cosmos.

参照 ▶ P72 作品 63
Work 63: refer to page 72

作品 24　かすみ草　ななかまど　コスモス
Work 24　Materials: Gypsophila, Mountain ash, Cosmos

作品 25　なんきんはぜ　椿　さんごアナナス
Work 25　Materials: Chinese tallow tree, Camellia, Aechmea fulgens (Aechmea)

なんきんはぜの枝と実の動きが吹き寄せる寒風を感じさせ、その空間に春へ向けて咲く椿を配しました。真っ赤なさんごアナナスで、明日への希望を表すとともに、色彩の対照効果を生み出しています。なんきんはぜの枝を交差させながら器にはめ込み、花留としました。

The dynamism of Chinese tallow branches and nuts give an image of a cold wind blowing. Within the space among the branches of such a harsh image, camellia is placed, blooming as it does, in spring. The red flowers of aechmea are symbolic of future hope, with a good color contrast. The *hanadome* (flower support) is the branches of the Chinese tallow tree, crossed and inserted into the bowl.

その他の水盤や広口の花器を用いた作品：
Other works using basin and bowl of wider opening:

作品17(P31)、作品56(P65)、作品60(P69)、作品61(P70)、作品63(P72)、作品64(P73)、作品65(P74)、作品90(P110)
Work 17 (page 31), Work 56 (page 65), Work 60 (page 69), Work 61 (page 70), Work 63 (page 72), Work 64 (page 73), Work 65 (page 74), Work 90 (page 110)

● 透明のガラス器を舞台として

　現代のいけばなでは、さまざまな色や形のガラス器が用いられています。透明のガラス器を用いると器の中の水も見え、花材のみずみずしさを高めてくれる効果が期待できます。一方で、器の中の花茎の見せ方や花留の工夫などが必要になります。

●Transparent glass as a stage

In contemporary ikebana, glassware of various colors and shapes are used. Using transparent glassware allows water inside the vessel to be seen, which can enhance the freshness of flower materials. On the other hand, the glassware requires suitable measures for how to display/conceal the flower stems in the vessel as well as the handling of *hanadome* (flower support).

作品 26　アジアンタム　ラン　ヘリコニア　アンスリウム　縞ふとい
Work 26　Materials: Maidenhair fern, Orchid, Heliconia, Anthurium, Scirpus tabernaemontani 'Zebrinus'

　らせんを描く鏡面仕上げの塩ビ板を花留としました。花器、花留、そして水の質感によって緑葉の美しさを表現した初夏の自由花です。1輪のランを花器の前面に配してアクセントとし、シャープな形に折り曲げた縞ふといでみずみずしいアジアンタムの柔らかさを際立たせました。

A twisted PVC sheet with a mirror finish is used as *hanadome* (flower support). This is a beautiful *jiyuka* evoking early summer, expressing the beauty of green leaves by the entire coordination of glass, *hanadome*, and presence of water. A single orchid is displayed on the front as a highlight, and the sharply bent Zebrinus effectively supports the lush taste of maidenhair fern.

折り曲げた縞ふといを吸盤で器に固定しました。色とりどりの草花を縞ふといの茎に挿し込んだり挟み込んだりして、それぞれの表情を生かしています。草花をリズムよく配し、夏のひとときの楽しさの中に涼感を求めました。

The bent Zebrinus is securely fixed in the glass bowl with suction cups. Various colors of flowers are inserted into the stems of Zebrinus for their optimum expression. The rhythmical arrangement of the flowers gives an image of happy summer days, with a sense of cool freshness.

作品 27　ナスタチウム　カラー　トルコぎきょう　縞ふとい
Work 27　Materials: Nasturtium, Calla, Prairie gentian, Scirpus tabernaemontani 'Zebrinus'

けむり草とミルクブッシュの枝を花器の底辺の一点から放射的に構成し、花留としています。八角蓮の緑葉を背景とし、色づいたけむり草のマッスに秋の訪れを感じる初秋の自由花です。

By arranging the branches of a smoke tree and milk bush radially from the bottom point of the vase, they are used as *hanadome* (flower support). With the green background of Chinese May Apple leaves, this is *jiyuka* for early autumn that announces the tell-tale dip in air temperature at this time via the mass of colors in the smoke tree.

作品 28　八角蓮　けむり草　アンスリウム　セイロンライティア　ミルクブッシュ
Work 28　Materials: Phodophillum pleianthum (Chinese May Apple), Smoke tree, Anthurium, Ceylon wrightia, Euphorbia tirucalli (milk bush)

参照 ▶ P71 作品62
Work 62: refer to page 71

星形の白いアマゾンリリーにクリスマスカラーの草花を取り合わせ、聖夜を表現しています。グラスを並べていけ、皆で集う一夜に飾る花です。グラスにはアマゾンリリーの茎だけを見せて、静寂を感じる「たて」の構成を強調しました。花留にはペットボトルを用いています。

White, star-shaped flowers of the Amazon lily are combined with the materials of Christmas colors, to express a holy night. Arranged glasses represent a night celebrated by friends and family gathered. By showing only the stems of Amazon lily in the glasses, the work emphasizes a vertical structure to give a silent impression. PET bottles are used as *hanadome* (flower support).

作品 29
アマゾンリリー　バラ　かすみ草
ヒペリクム　グリーントリフ
Work 29　Materials: Amazon lily, Rose, Gypsophila, Hypericum, Dianthus

---

その他の透明ガラス器を用いた作品：
Other works using transparent glassware

**作品55（P64）、作品57（P66）、
作品58（P67）、作品62（P71）、
作品63（P72）、作品77（P92）、
作品78（P93）、作品94（P114）、
作品106（P127）**

Work 55 (page 64), Work 57 (page 66),
Work 58 (page 67), Work 62 (page 71),
Work 63 (page 72), Work 77 (page 92),
Work 78 (page 93), Work 94 (page 114)
Work 106 (page 127),

● 生活雑器の活用

　食器などの普段から暮らしに用いているものは、違和感なく生活空間にマッチします。身の回りを見渡して、さまざまなものを自由花の器に活用してください。花留を工夫していけると、身近な生活雑器がおしゃれな花器に変身するでしょう。

•Utilizing everyday tableware

Containers in everyday use such as dishes will perfectly match our living space. Look around the rooms of your dwelling and see if you can find and use various items as attractive vessels for your *jiyuka*. Putting a little effort into a *hanadome* (flower support) will change the ordinary tableware into a splendid vessel.

作品 30　こでまり　フリージア　ヒューケラ
Work 30　Materials: Spiraea cantoniensis, Freesia, Heuchera

　信楽焼の酒器を活用しています。器の雰囲気に合わせて木を輪切りにしたプレートを敷き、そこに器を少し傾けて固定すると、「ちょっと一杯」の気分が演出できます。花器口の空間を見せながら軽やかにいけることがポイントです。

This work uses a sake holder and a cup made of Shigaraki-yaki. According to the mood created by the cup and the holder, a plate simulating a piece of cross-cut wood is laid down. Upon this a holder is fixed with a slightly tilted style which gives the inviting image of "Let's have a drink." A light, bright tone is required in this work; ensuring that there is enough space in the openings of the holder and the cup.

モルディブの市場で見つけた木製の食器にいけました。いたやかえでの枝を花留とし、水面をたっぷり見せることで、暑さの中のオアシスを表現しています。明るい色合いの南国風の敷物が濃い彩りの花と器を引き立たせる脇役となっています。

This work uses a wooden dish I found in a market in the Maldives. Using a maple branch as *hanadome* (flower support), the water surface is fully visible to express a cool oasis in the heat. A rag of bright tropical colors plays an effective role in highlighting dense colors of the flowers and the vessel.

作品 31 ジゴペタルム　いたやかえで
千日紅　寒すげ
Work 31　Materials: Zygopetalum orchid, Maple, Common globe amaranthus, sedge

白銀の季節に訪れた北欧で購入した食器に、春を待つ思いでいけた作品です。オリヅルランの広がる空間に、清らかな水仙の花を主役としました。また、その清らかさを白い器からのぞく水面で強調しています。

My feeling of "I can't wait for spring" is expressed in this work, in the tableware I bought in North Europe when I visited there in the snowy winter season. Within the space of the chlorophytum comosum, flowers of pure narcissus play the leading part. Such purity is further highlighted with a white-looking water surface in the white bowl.

作品 32　水仙　ぼけ
オリヅルラン　アンスリウム
Work 32　Materials: Narcissus, Japanese quince, Chlorophytum comosum, Anthurium

二つ並べたカップを花器とした食卓の花です。カップの金線模様に合わせて、金色のアルミ線を花留に用いました。鉄製の針金と異なり、アルミ線にはさびにくい特性があります。涼しげな緑葉を中心に初夏の花を添え、爽やかな季節感を捉えています。

Flower work on a table in a pair of cups. In keeping with the gold designs on the cups, gold aluminum wire is used as a *hanadome* (flower support). Aluminum wire is different to steel wire in that it is not prone to corrosion here. With a cool tone of green leaves in the center, flowers of the early summer season are added to frame a scene imbuing a refreshing seasonal feeling.

作品 33　カラディウム　バラ　てっせん
Work 33　　Materials: Caladium, Rose, Clematis

先輩教授からいただいたすてきなお茶わんに、お箸を花留にしていけました。お箸の両端を針金で固定していますが、一方は組みひもを巻いて空間のアクセントに。伸びやかなぼけの枝に柔らかなシクラメンを取り合わせた、春の自由花です。

In a beautiful bowl I was given by my senior professor, I made use of chopsticks as a *hanadome* (flower support) for the work. Both ends of the chopsticks were secured by wire, but for one of the ends I wound on a colorful string, *kumihimo*, to accentuate the space. This is *jiyuka* for the spring season, combining a lively branch of Japanese quince with the gentle tone of cyclamen flowers.

作品 34　ぼけ　シクラメン
Work 34　　Materials: Japanese quince, Cyclamen

作品 35　シクラメン　水仙　南天
Work 35　Materials: Cyclamen, Narcissus, Nandina

上海出張の際にいただいた小さな急須にいけました。シクラメンと水仙の花で明るく元気な生徒さんたちの笑顔を表現し、南天の葉の広がりで皆さんのご発展を祈念した作品です。

This work uses a small teapot, a *kyusu*, which I was given when I visited Shanghai. With flowers of cyclamen and narcissus I imagine happy and cheerful students in Shanghai, and with the stretching leaves of nandina I am optimistic for their future.

その他の生活雑器を用いた作品：
Other works using tableware:

作品10(P22)、作品11(P23)、作品29(P42)、作品54(P63)、作品55(P64)、作品58(P67)、作品59(P68)、作品62(P71)、作品78(P93)、作品82(P97)、作品93(P113)、作品95(P115)、作品96(P116)、作品98(P118)、作品99(P119)、作品100(P120)、作品101(P120)、作品103(P122)、作品106(P127)

Work 10 (page 22), Work 11 (page 23), Work 29 (page 42), Work 54 (page 63), Work 55 (page 64), Work 58 (page 67), Work 59 (page 68), Work 62 (page 71), Work 78 (page 93), Work 82 (page 97), Work 93 (page 113), Work 95 (page 115), Work 96 (page 116), Work 98 (page 118), Work 99 (page 119), Work 100 (page 120), Work 101 (page 120), Work 103 (page 122), Work 106 (page 127)

● 掛け花、釣り花

　床の間が減少傾向にある中、現代の花を飾る定番の場所であった玄関のげた箱も、最近のマンションなどでは床から天井まで壁面いっぱいの収納棚になりつつあります。このような環境の変化の中、掛けたりつったりして飾るいけばなの需要も高まりつつあります。また、掛けや釣りの自由花には、レリーフ、タペストリー、モビールという他の芸術分野からの構成法を取り入れたものもあります。

　これらレリーフ、タペストリー、モビールに共通する注意点は、いずれも池坊のいけばなであることを忘れてはならないということです。これは単にレリーフを制作することを目的とするのではなく、草木美を生かすことを最優先に考え、表現の先にレリーフがあるということです。従って、土台のデザインに凝り過ぎると花が不要になる恐れもあります。意外とシンプルな土台の方が花の美しさを生かしやすいものです。

・掛け花

　掛け花を大きく分類すると、①既成の器を壁面に掛けて花をいけるもの②自作の器や土台を壁に掛けて花をいけるもの③レリーフ④タペストリーの四つに分類できますが、いずれも池坊いけばなの伝統的美感と構成法に基づくものでなければなりません。つまり、レリーフやタペストリーといっても西洋芸術や西洋文化のそれらとは異なるものであり、他分野からヒントを得て、池坊の掛け花の幅を広げたものであると認識するべきです。

　植物を材料とした西洋芸術的なレリーフやモビールも考えられますが、専永家元の「形から姿へ」という方向性に基づく池坊のレリーフやタペストリーは、既成の花器や自作の器（土台）と同じく草木がドラマを演じる舞台や背景となり、草木の美しさを高めたり作品の表現を演出したりするものであると考える方が良いでしょう。常に草木美を生かすということを念頭に制作することが、池坊いけばなとして大切なことです。

● Hanging arrangement, Suspended arrangement

In the Japanese lifestyle these days, the *tokonoma* is gradually disappearing, and the ubiquitous shoe box in the entrance hall on which flowers have been commonly displayed now uses a different design that is paneled from the floor to the ceiling, so there is now no shelf. All of such situations reduce the possibilities for displaying flowers in our day-to-day lives. Here with ikebana, another style, hanging or suspended, is gaining popularity. Some of the *jiyuka* using the hanging or suspended style take the composition method from other artistic fields such as relief, tapestry, or mobiles.

Whether they are reliefs, tapestries, or mobile types, remember that they are common to Ikenobo Ikebana. In other words, the purpose of making a relief is not making an art work, but to prioritize the beauty of plants. When we become too distracted by the base design, sometimes there will be no need for flowers. Remarkably, the simplest base can often draw out the beauty of the flowers.

・Hanging arrangement

There are four main categories for hanging arrangement: 1) Flowers in a conventional vase hang on a wall, 2) Flowers in a vase or base originally made and hang on a wall, 3) Relief, 4) Tapestry. All of them must be based on the traditional aesthetic and structural methods of Ikenobo. In other words, the words "relief" and "tapestry" are not those commonly recognized as western art or designs. It must be recognized as something developed from Ikenobo hanging style, inspired by the other cultural fields.

You may feel the western style of relief or mobile is possible as long as they use greens or plants as materials; the Ikenobo reliefs or tapestries based on the concept "From shape to style" advocated by the Headmaster Sen'ei Ikenobo should be, however, as well as the conventional or original vases (bases), the stage or the backgrounds for the plants to play a drama. Everything is just for enhancing the beauty of plants or directing to express the maximum of work impression. The beauty of plants first—it is the core of Ikenobo Ikebana in creating a work.

作品 36　秋明菊　やまほろし　りんどう　ミスカンツス
Work 36　Materials: Japanese anemone, Solanum japonense (potato vine), Gentian, Miscanthus

置きと掛け・釣りとの相違の一つは、花器口の下の空間です。掛け花や釣り花では、花器口より下の空間を生かして草木の軽やかな美しさを表現することが基本です。この作品では、凛と咲く秋明菊を中心に、やまほろしとミスカンツスのなびきを生かし、秋風を捉えました。

One significant difference between the three ikebana styles: standing, hanging, and suspended, is the space under the vase opening. In the hanging or suspended styles, basically the work utilizes a space below the vase opening to express the airy allure of the plants. This work focuses the Japanese anemone with its dignified strength, supported by the bowing of the potato vine and miscanthus, to express an autumn wind.

黒く着色したキーウィづるを構成し、銀の花入れを中心に配して舞台とします。無機質でモノトーンな舞台に、草花の柔らかな質感を生かして軽やかに構成し、赤いヘリコニアで作品を引き締めました。

Organized as a black-painted kiwi vine, a silver vase, which is the stage, is located in the center. The inorganic and monotone style of the stage is mixed with the soft, elegant texture of the flowers, summarized in a light, vivacious tone. A red heliconia adds an interesting accent to the work.

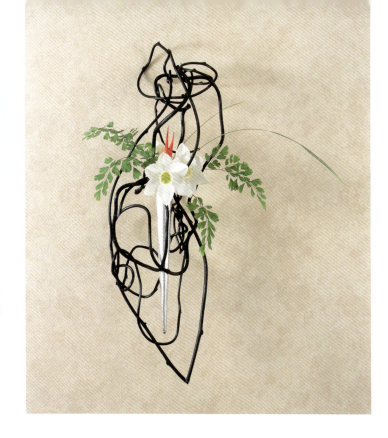

作品 37　アマゾンリリー　アジアンタム　ヘリコニア　ミスカンツス　キーウィづる
Work 37　Materials: Amazon lily, Maidenhair fern, Heliconia, Miscanthus, Kiwi vine

かつて池坊アメリカ事務所の所在地であった「霧のサンフランシスコ」がテーマです。池坊のロゴ入りコースターをあの有名な吊り橋・金門橋（ゴールデンゲートブリッジ）のようにデザインしました。霧に煙る金門橋と「あじさい坂」として知られる名所・ロンバート通りは、私の大好きな場所でした。コースターの一部をカットして配することで、額の外へと続いていく動きを感じさせます。

The topic of this work is "Misty San Francisco," the previous location of the Ikenobo America Office. The coasters are arranged so that they represent the Golden Gate Bridge. The misty Golden Gate Bridge and Lombard Street popular for its hydrangea bushes are both my favorites. An array of partially cut coasters gives a sequential rhythm to the work not bounded by the frame.

作品 38　ブルーハイビスカス　けむり草　あじさい
Work 38　Materials: Lilac hibiscus, smoke tree, Hydrangea

黒の土台にステンレスのドアの取っ手と花入れをたてに配して、シンプルな空間を作りました。「たて」の構成が花材の広がる動きを際立たせています。「雨宿り」をテーマとして、梅雨の合間の清涼感を捉えた掛け花です。

On a black base, stainless door handles and a vase are vertically aligned for a simple and straightforward mood of space. This vertical structure highlights the stretching 'motion' of the floral materials. A fresh, vivid hanging arrangement suggesting a moment in a rain shelter during the rainy season.

作品39　パフィオペディルム　アンスリウム
日々草　ういきょう　アンペライ

Work 39　Materials: Paphiopedilum orchid, Anthurium, Madagascar periwinkle, Fennel, Machaerina rubiginosa

木製のお盆に紅葉の写真を貼って土台としました。花入れにも写真を貼って土台と同化させ、お盆と写真の端に黒いテープを貼って空間を引き締めました。紅葉を背景として秋草を軽やかにいけた、季節感を楽しむ掛け花です。

A wooden base is used, with a picture of colored leaves pasted on to it. The holders are also pasted on within the same picture, so that they appear assimilated with the base. The black tape is applied at each side edge of the base and the picture to show separation of the areas, and which sharpens the entire tone of the work. This is a hanging-style work of autumn flowers with colored leaves in the background, for a vivid seasonal feel.

作品40　ききょう　えのころ草
おみなえし　セイロンライティア　花とうがらし

Work 40　Materials: Japanese bellflower, Foxtail grass, Patrinia scabiosifolia, Ceylon wrightia, Capsicum

茶色の布地に、東南アジアで求めた木製のフォークとスプーンを取り付けたタペストリーです。花入れには木製のランチョンマットを切ったものを巻いて、同系色の舞台としました。夏の朝のダイニングルームにいかがでしょうか。

A tapestry made of a brown cloth, on which is placed a wooden spoon and fork that were bought in East Asia. A wooden luncheon mat is cut and wound around the vase, and a stage of the same color tone is used. An ideal work for a dining room display on a summer morning.

作品 41　ハイビスカス　オンシディウム　カラテア　せきしょう
Work 41　Materials: Hibiscus, Oncidium orchid, Calathea, Acorus gramineus

作品 42 ひもげいとう ほととぎす ミラ
Work 42 Materials: Amaranthus, Japanese toad lily, Milla biflora

軽やかさを感じることがタペストリーの特徴です。この作品では、淡い緑のランチョンマットを土台として活用しました。秋草を取り合せた初秋の花ですが、初夏の花も合いそうです。季節に合わせた草花を軽やかにいけて飾る暮らしの花です。

A key feature of the tapestry work is its airiness. This work uses a light green luncheon mat as the base. Here, early autumn flowers are used, but those of early summer might look wonderful, too. This is an everyday flower work tailored to the season—casual but spontaneous.

> その他の掛け花作品：
> Other hanging works:
>
> 作品49（P58）、作品51（P59）、作品52（P60）、作品82（P97）、作品89（P109）
>
> Work 49 (page 58), Work 51 (page 59), Work 52 (page 60), Work 82 (page 97), Work 89 (page 109)

・釣り花

　釣り花は、①既成の器をつるもの②自作の器や土台をつるもの③モビールの三つに分類されます。掛け花のレリーフやタペストリーと同じく、モビールも池坊の釣り花の幅を広げるために西洋芸術から取り入れられた構成法の一つであり、モビールそのものよりも自然の草木の美しさをいけることが大切であると思います。つまり池坊のモビールとは、空気の動きによって作品に動く要素が加わり、草木に求める美しさを高める構成法の一つだといえます。

・ **Suspended arrangement**

Suspended style is categorized into three groups: 1) suspending of conventional vases, 2) suspending of handmade vases or vessels, and 3) Mobiles. Just as reliefs or tapestries of the hanging style, mobiles are one of the organizational approaches taken from the western arts to garner a wider understanding of Ikenobo suspended works. Again, the mobile work in Ikenobo should focus in the beauty of natural plants rather than the mobile itself. The Ikenobo mobiles are an option in ikebana organizational approaches to further draw out the beauty of flowers by air flow giving another element of "motion" to the work.

作品43　日々草　われもこう
Work 43　Materials: Madagascar periwinkle, Great burnet

ヤシの葉柄から舟をイメージした釣り花です。生花の伝花に出船、入船、泊船がありますが、停泊を意味する泊船は置き生です。つることによって動感を演出する池坊の伝統から学び、この作品では舟が行き交う情景を表現しました。日々草の枝ぶりを生かした軽やかな釣り花です。

A suspended work imagining boats from the shape of palm husks. The traditional *shoka* style has three styles using "boat-shaped" vessels: *De-bune* (outgoing boats), *Iri-bune* (entering boats), and *Tomari-bune* (boats stopping). The *Tomari-bune*, which means laid at anchor, is a standing ikebana style. Suspending this style of work can produce dynamism, which was a traditionally-recognized style in Ikenobo. This work expresses a scene of boats passing. With the Madagascar periwinkle cascading, the work shows an ethereal, fresh taste.

作品 44　山しだ　てっせん　バラ
Work 44　Materials: Dicranopteris linearis (fern), Clematis, Rose

竹でモビールの舞台を作りました。つなぎ手に釣り糸を用いることはよくありますが、見える部分はすべて作品の一部です。この作品では、統一感を求めててっせんの色と同調する組みひもを使いました。風に揺れる山しだに初夏の花を出合わせ、季節の情感を映しています。

The stage of the mobile is made from bamboo. One of common connection wires is a fishing line, but don't forget that everything seen from outside is part of the work. Here braided cords are used, for consistency and harmonization of the color tone with that of clematis. The swaying ferns meet the flowers of early summer, expressing the season's sentiment.

作品 45　ききょう　ラン　クロトン　おみなえし　菊
Work 45　Materials: Japanese bellflower, Orchid, Croton, Patrinia scabiosifolia, Chrysanthemum

何段にも構成することがグレードの高いモビールの条件というわけではなく、表現のための構成であることが大切です。作品では、釣り花に祇園祭のうちわを取り合わせ、動く要素によって夏のお祭りに涼感を求めました。また、その下に同じ器を置いていけ、上下の関連性を持たせています。祇園祭が終われば立秋も間近。夏から秋への季(とき)の移りを捉えています。

An excellent mobile work does not mean a complex technique made of many stages of structuring; a mobile needs to be just an option for advanced expression. This work combines the suspended arrangement with a fan from the Gion festival pattern, in which the dynamic element expresses the summer festival with a cool impression. The same vase is placed under this suspended work for a linked story. When the Gion festival passes, the season is headed for early autumn. This work is meant to catch the seasonal shift from summer to autumn.

作品 46　グロリオサ　ミラ　玉しだ　シクラメン
Work 46　Materials: Gloriosa, Milla biflora, Sword fern, Cyclamen

花の周囲にクリスマスツリーを飾る玉を配したモビールです。赤いグロリオサにろうそくの炎をイメージしました。空間を引き締めるために黒いアクリル板を用いていますが、この板が空気の動きを捉えることによってモビールの動きが強まります。

A mobile arranged with Christmas ornaments around the flowers. Red flowers of gloriosa represent candle flames. A black acrylic plate plays the role of sharpening the entire tone; the moving of the plate according to the air flow gives an interesting accent to the mobile.

その他の釣り花作品:
Other suspended works:

作品47(P57)、作品48(P58)、作品53(P61)、作品77(P92)、作品91(P111)

Work 47 (page 57), Work 48 (page 58), Work 53 (page 61), Work 77 (page 92), Work 91 (page 111)

● 木枠を活用して

　草木が演じるドラマの舞台の一つとして、衝立や屏風のような枠の活用が考えられます。本書では、白木の枠を用いた作品を何作か紹介していますが、飾る環境や表現に応じてはアルミのような金属の枠を作ってドラマの舞台とするのも良いでしょう。また、複数の枠を用いることによって作品のサイズを調節することもできます。

●Using a wooden frame

As a stage for plants to play out a drama, a frame such as a partition or *byobu* is helpful. In this book, some works using plain wood are introduced; depending on the place for display or the expression intended, a metallic frame such as an aluminum frame can be used. More than one frame is also possible to adjust the size of the work.

作品 47　あじさい　けむり草　てっせん　姫ゆり
Work 47　Materials: Hydrangea, Smoke tree, Clematis, Star lily

　木枠の空間に花器をつった釣り花です。同季の花材を取り合わせた初夏の花ですが、つることで爽やかな軽やかさを演出しています。

A suspended work with the vases suspended in the space made by a wooden frame. Representing early summer by way of the season's flower materials, the work, when suspended, improves its fresh tone.

白い竹の器に合わせ、枠の中に白竹を配して空間を分割しています。たてに配した竹が花材の広がりと立体感を引き立たせる構成です。前作では、花材の色に合わせた組みひもをつなぎ手に使用しましたが、この作品では竹の「たて」の構成を強調するために透明な釣り糸を用いています。

The white bamboo is positioned in the frame harmonizing with the white bamboo vases and delineating space. Vertical lines of bamboo enhance the stretching of flowers, contributing to a solid appearance. The previous work used braided cords of colors similar to the flowers, while this work uses transparent fishing line to accentuate the vertical bamboo structure.

作品 48　ラン　トルコぎきょう　山ごぼう　ゴッドセフィアナ
Work 48　Materials: Orchid, Prairie gentian, Phytolacca Americana, Dracaena

枠の中に板を配して掛け花の要領でいけています。暗色の板を背景として、花材のエネルギッシュな色彩を際立たせました。また、力強さを求めて、線的な花材を用いずに構成しています。この作品に限らず、「点」「線」「面」「マッス」はそれぞれの働きを考えて用いなければなりません。

The plate is positioned in a frame, using a hanging work style. With the dark color plate in the background, the energetic colors of the floral materials are highlighted. For strength and power, the work is formed without depending on the linear shapes of the plants. Not only in this work, but in many others, too, we usually have to consider the role that each of the points, lines, surface, and mass plays.

作品 49　ひまわり　モンステラ　日々草
Work 49　Materials: Sunflower, Monstera, Madagascar periwinkle

蓮のみを用いた作品です。存在感ある開花をあえて用いず、蕾と蓮肉、巻葉と開葉と朽葉で構成し、過去、現在、未来の移り変わりを静けさの中に捉えました。苔を付けたネットを背景に配して、枯れた蓮肉が宙に昇っていくように見せています。

This work uses only lotus. Because of not using a blooming flower, which gives an impression of presence, buds, fruits, and different appearances of leaves are used (curled up, open, and decaying) so that the work can express the time of change—past, present, and future in a quiet scene. The mossy net behind is intended to give an impression that the decaying lotus fruit is moving up in the air.

作品 50　蓮
Work 50　Materials: Lotus

作品48の釣り花で用いた白竹の器を枠の中心に用いた掛け花です。枠に和紙調の塩ビ板を貼り、竹と金紙でデザインしています。そのデザインに合わせて、紅白の花の彩りと緑の広がりを生かしました。

This hanging work positions the white bamboo vase used in the suspended work 48 in the center of the frame. A PVC plate of Japanese *washi* paper is pasted on the frame, and decorated with bamboo and golden paper. According to the desired stage setting, use was made of the red-and-white flower colors and a spread of green.

作品 51　ラン　ゴッドセフィアナ　アスパラガス　アンスリウム
Work 51　Materials: Orchid, Dracaena, Asparagus, Anthurium

作品 52 　てっせん　カラディウム　オクロレウカ
Work 52　Materials: Clematis, Caladium, Iris ochroleuca

和紙調の塩ビ板をカットして空間を作り、その空間に緑が立ち伸びる美しさを捉えました。紫のてっせんを取り合わせ、涼感を表現しています。緑葉の連動を生かすために花入れの白竹を木枠の上から下まで取り付け、部分的に穴を開けていけました。

A PVC sheet laminated with Japanese *washi* paper is cut to make a space, in which the beauty of the growing greenery is captured. Purple clematis flowers are coordinated for coolness. To effectively show the sequential, linked image of green leaves, the slender vase of white bamboo is attached from the top to the base of the wooden frame, with openings at some parts in the center.

二つの木枠を組み合わせたセンターピースの作品です。センターピースの作品は、裏表がはっきりしない花や葉を取り合わせることが基本的なポイントです。作品では、グロリオサの表情を生かし、軽やかなアスパラガスの動きを添えています。このように、複数の木枠を組み合わせることによって、さまざまな構成が可能になります。

A centerpiece work combining two wooden frames. This work needs to have the flowers and the leaves with no distinct front and rear patterns. The work leverages the impression of gloriosa, adding an airy movement of asparagus. Like this, combining dual wooden frames facilitates various other compositions.

作品 53 グロリオサ　アスパラガス
かすみ草　ゴッドセフィアナ　バラ
Work 53　Materials: Gloriosa, Asparagus, Gypsophila, Dracaena, Rose

ドラマの演出
● 花留の工夫

立花で用いる込み藁(わら)は、器に花材をしっかりと立てるために先人が考え出した花留の工夫です。近代では剣山も考案され、自由花ではフラワーアレンジメント用に開発された吸水性スポンジも重宝されています。

自由花では目に見える部分すべてが作品の一部であり、表現や制作意図に応じて多種多様な器を用います。このことから花留の工夫も必要となってきます。花留を見せない工夫や、逆に花留を見せることで作品の一部として働かせる工夫です。

本書では、ペットボトルなどの身近な素材を用いた花留も紹介しています。

Directions for making a drama
●*Hanadome (flower support) technique*

The *komiwara* (inserted straw) used in *rikka* is a *hanadome* technique devised by the ancient masters to secure the floral materials in vases. In modern times *kenzan* was invented, and the water-absorbent sponges developed for floral arrangements are also popularly used in ikebana.

In *jiyuka*, everything seen is a part of the work; according to the expression or intended performance, many varieties of vases are used. This then requires an effective use or technique of *hanadome*. The methods for making visible or invisible *hanadome* are more useful tips to know.

This book refers to *hanadome* using ordinary and common materials such as PET bottles.

この木蓮に出合った時、まろやかな枝ぶりとふくよかな開花に、3人の男の子を育てている肝っ玉母さんを連想しました。木蓮の空間に子どもたちをイメージした3輪の都忘れを配して温もりのある家庭を表現しました。花留は木蓮の枝を利用しています。

This magnolia tree with its round branches and rich, plump blossom, reminded me of a loving mother of experience. The mother perhaps brought up three sons with care and also with toughness. By carefully arranging three aster flowers, a heartwarming home is expressed. The flowers are secured by using a fork-shaped magnolia branch.

作品 54　木蓮　都忘れ
work 54　Materials: Magnolia, Miyamayomena savatieri (aster)

作品 55 ダリア　パンジー
Work 55 Materials: Dahlia, Pansy

二人のお姉ちゃんと一緒にポーズする男の子をイメージしました。塩ビ板に穴を開けたものを花留としています。たった3本の作品ですが、一輪一輪の花と葉の表情、そして三つの花の空間に注意しました。明るい色合いの敷物で子どもたちのかわいらしさを演出しています。

I imagined a boy standing with his two elder sisters. As a *hanadome* (flower support), a PVC plate with holes is used. Although this work uses only three seedlings, impressions are given by each of the flowers and the leaves, along with the space between them, these are well considered. A cloth of bright color tone expresses the cute impression of "the children."

作品 56　コスモス
Work 56　Materials: Cosmos

黒いガラス器でコスモスの自然な表情と彩りを生かした作品です。ゆったりした雰囲気を求めて挿し口を分割しました。花留は、吸盤に通して器に固定したアルミ線の先にコスモスを挿しています。

The black glassware highlights the natural elegance of the cosmos flowers with their colors. For a relaxing tone, they are separately positioned. The *hanadome* (flower support), the aluminum wire threaded through the suction cups, is secured with the vase, onto which the flowers are arranged.

作品 57 　トルコぎきょう　バラ
Work 57 　Materials: Prairie gentian, Rose

サイコロ型の透明ガラス器に鏡面仕上げの塩ビ板を2枚はめ込み、その間に花を挿して器の中の花茎が見えないように工夫しています。銀色の敷板を用いて塩ビ板と同調させ、草花のみずみずしさを引き立たせました。

In the dice-shaped transparent glass vase, two mirror-finish PVC sheets are inserted. Between the plates the flowers are inserted so that the stems inside the glass vase are not visible. A silver plate is laid under the vase to harmonize the color of the PVC sheets, bringing out the fresh appearance of the flowers.

作品 58　グロリオサ　セイロンライティア　縞ふとい
Work 58　Materials: Gloriosa, Ceylon wrightia, Scirpus tabernaemontani 'Zebrinus'

前作と同じ手法ですが、この作品では透明の塩ビ板を用いて器の中の花茎を見せています。水中で花が自立しているように見せ、伸びやかさを求めました。折り曲げた縞ふといの空間で、大小2輪の花の美しさを際立たせています。

The same technique that was used in the previous work is used, but in this case the flower stems in the glass are shown, by using a transparent PVC sheet. This helps the appearance of the flowers standing independently in the water, expressing further growing energy. The bend of the Zebrinus creates a space which highlights the beauty of two flowers with their contrasting size.

作品 59　コチョウラン　バラ　あじさい
Work 59　Materials: Phalaenopsis aphrodite orchid, Rose, Hydrangea

ガラスのろうそく入れを器として、事務用のクリップを花留に活用しました。クリップに挿し込んで花を留めることで水面を見せ、光を通すガラス器の美しさを生かしています。あじさいの緑葉でコチョウランの動きとバランスを取るのが構成のポイントです。

In a vase of a glass candle case, office paper clips are used for *hanadome* (flower support). The flowers are secured by inserting into the clips, which allows the water surface to be seen and enhance the beauty of glassware through which the light passes. The green leaves of Hydrangea help to keep balance with the outstretched phalaenopsis aphrodite orchid flowers, which is the key technique of this work.

作品 60 サンダーソニア　コスモス　レクス・ベゴニア
Work 60 Materials: Sandersonia, Cosmos, Begonia

涼しげなガラスの水盤の模様を生かした作品です。石や剣山を使うと、せっかくの器の模様が消えてしまうので、透明なペットボトルの底に穴を開けたものを吸盤で固定して花を留めています。

To effectively show the cool taste of the pattern of the glass basin, for *hanadome* (flower support) a transparent PET bottle, after making holes in its base, is secured by a suction cup. Note that using pebbles or *kenzan* instead would hide these beautiful patterns.

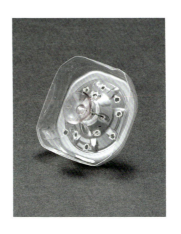

作品 61　カラー　アジアンタム　レウココリネ
Work 61　Materials: Calla, Maidenhair fern, Leucocoryne

作品 60 では、花留が見えないように透明のペットボトルを用いましたが、この作品では水面が光り輝くように細く切った鏡面仕上げの塩ビ板を結んで花留にしました。花留のきらきら感が草花の美しさを高めています。

In work 60 a transparent pet bottle is used for hiding *hanadome* (flower support). This work, however, uses a tied PVC sheet, mirror finish, after cutting it thin so that the water surface shines brightly. The shiny appearance of this *hanadome* increases the beauty of flowers.

作品 62　ラッパ水仙　スプレンゲリ　バラ　パンジー
Work 62　Materials: Daffodil, Asparagus 'Splengeri', Rose, pansy

春の歓送迎会に飾る花として、皆で乾杯するグラスを用いました。前作と同じ手法の花留ですが、器の透明感を生かすためにペットボトルを細く切ったものを結んで留めています。ラッパ水仙の広がりを強調するため、敷物で花の下の空間を引き締めました。

For welcome or farewell parties common in spring in Japan, the work uses glasses for conveying cheerfulness. The same technique of *hanadome* (flower support) as that of the previous work is used, but this time the PET bottles are cut into thin pieces to improve transparency when used with the glassware. To emphasize the spreading daffodil flowers, a cloth is laid under the glasses, which accentuates the space under the flowers.

作品 63 　グロリオサ　コスモス　アスパラガス
Work 63 　Materials: Gloriosa, Cosmos, Asparagus

かわいい食卓の花です。グロリオサは、器の壁面に吸盤を取り付け、その穴に挿し込んで留めています。さらに、器にアスパラガスを浮かべ、その緑のマッスにコスモスを挿して留めました。剣山などを使用しないことで、食卓の清潔感を保つ工夫です。

This is a work of cute flowers on a dining table. The gloriosa flowers are secured by inserting them into a hole made in a suction cup on the inner wall of the glass bowl. Asparagus leaves are "floated" on the bowl, and the cosmos flowers are secured by inserting them into the green mass. Avoiding use of *kenzan* or other *hanadome* (flower support) tools helps keep the clean image of the work for a table.

作品 64　カーネーション　日々草　バラ　レクス・ベゴニア
Work 64　Materials: Carnation, Madagascar periwinkle, Rose, Begonia

網目状のプラスチック製の円筒を花器に固定して花留としました。円筒の色と同系色のカーネーションを主役とし、小さな花を取り合わせて主役に広がりを持たせました。茎や葉に針金を添えないことで、レクス・ベゴニアのような葉も長持ちします。

The plastic tubular mesh is fixed to the bowl for *hanadome* (flower support). The carnation flowers of the same color of the cylinder plays a main role, to which the combination of small flowers gives an accent. No metal wire on or around the stem or leaves can keep the begonia leaves long.

作品 65 けむり草　ベルてっせん　むくげ

Work 65　Materials: Smoke tree, Clematis, Hibiscus syriacus

けむり草の枝の交差を針金で結んで立たせています。てっせんは、茎に針金を添えたりせず、花の表情を見ながらけむり草に茎を絡ませて留めました。安易に針金を添えると、見る人が癒やされません。手法に依存し過ぎず、自然な美しさを生かすことが大切です。

Crossed smoke tree branches are tied with metal wire, to support the branches so that they stand upright. As for clematis flowers, instead of fixing them with wire, the stems are secured by twisting them around the smoke tree branches to obtain the best orientation of the blossoms. Casual adding of wire can kill the mood of the work, giving an uneasy, savage impression. It is important to seek how we can fully draw out natural beauty without depending too much on physical supporting techniques.

● 敷物の活用

立花や生花は敷板の上に飾ることがよくありますが、自由花においても飾る環境との調和やドラマの演出の一つとして、敷板やランチョンマットのような敷物を活用する場合があります。例えば、ミニチュア自由花でよく敷物を用いるのは、小さな作品に存在感と安定感を与える目的があるからです。表現や構成、さらには飾る環境に応じて工夫しましょう。

● Using a board and a cloth

Rikka or *shoka* commonly use a wooden board under the vase. In *jiyuka*, too, to harmonize with the display space or as one of the tools for dramatic expression, a board or a cloth, such as a sheet, luncheon mat, is useful. For example, we popularly use a rag in miniature *jiyuka*, because by doing this we can make a small work visually more stable and give it a more powerful presence. A board or a cloth can be optionally used according to the expression, structure, or a display space.

ガラスの丸い器にランの表情を捉え、下葉を省略した玉しだで動きを与えています。敷物なしの場合と2通りの敷物を用いた場合の3枚の写真を見比べてください。敷物によって安定感が増しますが、その形によっても花の見え方が変わります。

Within a round glass vase, the impressive tone of orchid flowers is positioned, with the balance of sword fern branches of which the lower leaves are removed to strengthen the dynamism. Compare three pictures: with two types of sheet, and without a sheet. The sheet increases the stable tone, but according to the shape, the flowers look different.

作品66 ラン バラ ヒューケラ 玉しだ
Work 66 Materials: Orchid, Rose, Heuchera, Sword fern

作品 67 ミルトニア　オンシディウム　しだ　りんどう
Work 67 Materials: Miltonia orchid, Oncidium orchid, Fern, Gentian

ミルトニアの表情を生かして、三つの器にそれぞれをいけることで、皆でダンスを踊っているようなイメージでいけました。黒い板を敷くと全体がまとまって見えますが、求める効果によっては敷物の有無や用い方を考える必要があります。

According to the impression of each miltonia orchid flower, each flower is separately put into a vase. This gives the impression that three of them are dancing together. Placing a black sheet under the work would help to add a consistent tone to the entire work, but it depends on what is the desired expression and in what way it should be achieved; using or not using a sheet, and which type of sheet should be used, is also an important option for effectively expressing the work.

第三章 自由花の楽しみ方

自由花制作のプロセス：『池坊いけばな自由花入門カリキュラム』の活用

● 制作のプロセス＝①発想（きっかけ）→ ②表現の設定→ ③素材の調達→
　　　　　　　　④構成の決定→ ⑤手法の選択

①自由花を制作する時、変わったことをしようと変形などの手法から考え始める人がいますが、自由花とは変わった作品をつくることではありません。自由花とは、素直な思いで草木と向き合って何らかの美を見いだし、形式にとらわれることなく、その美しさを生かしながら意図する表現に基づいて構成するいけばななのです。

②そこで、何よりも発想に基づく表現設定が重要となります。発想という言葉には難しい響きがあるかもしれませんが、もっと肩の力を抜いて花とのふれあいを楽しんでください。また、自由花も伝統ある池坊いけばなの様式の一つなので、つくることばかり考えずに、いけばなの原点である「いける」ということをいつも認識するべきです。いけばな作品に対する発想とは、花をいけるきっかけともいえます。素直な気持ちで花と向き合えば、もっと自由花の楽しさが感じられるはずです。

③さて、作品を通した表現（ドラマ）が決まったら、次にそのドラマの役者となる花材と舞台となる器や土台の選択作業となります。花との出合い、花とのふれあいがいけばなの原点であることから、たまたま出合った花の何を生かすかが表現内容となることもあります。その場合は、ドラマの主役が決定したわけですから、舞台はその主役や表現に応じた他の花材や花器の取り合わせということになります。

④表現内容が決まって、役者（花材）と舞台（器や土台）がそろったら、いよいよ制作開始です。まずは構成を考えましょう。構成については、大きく分けて「置く」「掛ける」「釣る」の三つに分類されます。さらに、「たて」「ななめ」「よこ」のいずれかにまとめることを考えましょう。この「たて」「ななめ」「よこ」は、表現に応じた構成のためのおおまかな目安であって、型というわけではありません。花材を無理やり「たて」や「よこ」に当てはめることがないよう注意してください。また、「たて」「ななめ」あるいは「よこ」にまとめる中で、前述のような「際立てる」ということも考えなければいけません。いわゆる対照効果を大切にしましょう。

⑤次に、制作過程においては、さまざまな手法を駆使する場合があります。例えば、表現に応じた花材の変形などの手法を取り入れることもあります。ただし、花材を変形する際は、あくまでも表現に応じた目的意識を持ち、花材を傷めるだけの過度な変形にならないよう注意しましょう。

「自由花だから変形」というような考え方では、単に変わった作品になるだけで、言い換えれば「変ないけばな」になってしまいます。また、花器の形に合わせて花材を変形しようとする人もいますが、花器と花材の形を合わせることが自由花の目的ではありません。草木美を生かした表現の過程の中で花器と花材の調和を考えることが大切です。さらに、制作の過程においては、花留の工夫も表現に応じた手法の一つといえます。

表現と素材の取り合わせ

「自由花とは、花に意味を与えること」という教えがあります。これは、作者の思いに基づいて、それぞれの花材に役割を与えることを意味します。そして、作品制作を通して一つのドラマを作り上げる過程においては、花材を「主役」「相手役」「脇役」に分類することができます。

「主役」とは、当然ながら表現の中心的存在になるものですが、「相手役」の選び方が重要となります。「相手役」とは、二番目に好きな花材や単に二番目に用いた花材ではなく、「主役」との対照効果を持つものでなければなりません。対照美こそが「和の精神」に基づく池坊いけばなとして大切なことです。この「主役」と「相手役」の関係は、新風体における「主＝主役」と「用＝主と対応するもの」の関係ともいえます。

「脇役」は、「あしらい」です。「あしらい」とはサプリメントのようなものです。健康を維持するためのさまざまなサプリメントが世に存在する昨今ですが、自分の健康のために必要なサプリメントを摂取することが大切であって、サプリメントを摂取し過ぎるとかえって健康を損なうかもしれません。作品構成においても同じことがいえます。表現や構成に不必要な花材を加えてしまうと、せっかくの作品が台無しになってしまいます。

「和の精神」に基づく池坊いけばなとしては、「主役」と「相手役」の対照美や相乗効果が重要であり、もし両者による構成だけで求める表現が成し遂げられたならば、サプリメント（「あしらい」「脇役」）は必要ないことになります。しかし、現実的には、作品の意図を深めるために何らかのサプリメントが必要になることが多くあります。いわゆる、果たすべき役割を持った「脇役」（あしらい）が必要となるのです。

3種類目以降の「脇役」の選択と用い方においては、「何のため」という目的意識を持つことが大切です。「これも好きな花だから」といった用い方は絶対にやめましょう。せっかくの作品が「好きな花の盛り合わせ」になってしまいます。

Chapter 3 How to Enjoy *Jiyuka*

Process of creating *Jiyuka*: Utilizing the "Ikenobo Ikebana An Introductory Free Style Curriculum"

- **Process of creation: motif or idea (cue) → deciding upon an expression → preparing materials → deciding upon a structure → selecting a method**

1) When creating *jiyuka*, some people start from planning the method, such as transformation of the material to

create a unique work. However, *jiyuka* are not unique arrangements. It is the ikebana way to structure it depending on the intended expression, while finding the beauty of plants by communicating using them with an honest heart, enhancing the appeal without being caught in existing rules on the shape.

2) What is most important is to decide upon an expression based on the motif or idea. The term "motif" might be a difficult to imagine, and to help with this you should just enjoy the interaction with flowers while having a relaxed attitude. Also, you should always think about "*ikeru,*" which is part of the basics of ikebana, not just to create a work, because *jiyuka* is also one of the styles of traditional Ikenobo Ikebana. The motif for a work of ikebana is a cue to arrange flowers. When you communicate with flowers with an honest heart, you can enjoy *jiyuka* more.

3) Once the expression target (the drama) for the work is decided, you now have to select the material flowers, then the performers of the drama, and the vase, which is the stage of the drama. The original point of the ikebana is the encounter with the flowers and interaction with them. What aspect of the flowers you happened to encounter can be the expression of the work. Now once you found the main character of the drama, you have to select other material flowers and a vessel depending on the desired final character and expression.

4) Expression is now decided, and performers (material flowers) and the stage (vase or base) are ready. Now, it is time to begin the creation. First, let's select the structure. Structures can be roughly classified into three types; "standing, hanging, and suspended." Also, you have to consider the orientation to apply to your work from among "vertical," "slanting," and "horizontal." These orientations are just rough indications and not formal styles. You should not forcibly fit your work into one of these orientations, rather use them as a guide. Moreover, you have to consider "emphasizing," as mentioned above, while you plan the orientation. So-called contrasting effect is very important.

5) We can use various methods in the process of creation. For example, we can use the method to reshape, or modify, the material depending on the expression. However, you must always have a purpose based on the expression when reshaping materials, and you must not reshape them so much so that they become damaged. The idea of "Free Style" does not mean "to reshape the material" and excessive action here will just make your work strange. In other words, it ends up being a "weird ikebana." Some people try to reshape the material to fit the shape of vessel, but fitting the material to the vessel is not the goal of *jiyuka*. It is important to consider the harmony of flowers and vessels while enhancing the natural beauty of the plants. Being creative about how to secure the flowers is also one of the methods of arranging the work, depending on the expression.

How to Select Material Flowers

There is a lesson, "*Jiyuka* is to give meaning to the flowers" which means to assign a role to each flower based on the thoughts of the creator. In the process of making a drama through creation of a work, we can classify material flowers into "main character," "responding character," and "supporting character."

The "main character" is of course the one to be the center of the expression, however the more important point is the selection the "responding character." This character is not just your second favorite material flower nor the one you added in the arrangement second in order. It has to have a contrasting effect against the "main character." The contrasting effect is the most important point of Ikenobo Ikebana, which is based on "the spirit of harmony." We can say that the relationship between the "main character" and the "responding character" is same as the relationship between "*shu*: main character" and "*yo*: the character responding *shu*" in *shimputai*.

"Supporting character" is "*ashirai,*" and it is just like a supplement. There have been a lot of supplements introduced to maintain our health nowadays. However, it is important to realize that in the same way that each person has his or her own unique supplement requirements which if exceeded may lead to many problems so, it is for the structure of arrangement. Adding material flowers unnecessary or inappropriate for the expression or structure will spoil the whole effect.

For Ikenobo Ikebana, which based on the "Spirit of harmony," the beauty of the contrast and synergistic effect of the relationship between the "main character" and "responding character" is the most important point. If a structure with only two of these elements can complete the expression, the additional supplement ("*ashirai*" or "supporting character") is not necessary. Realistically speaking, however, it is often the case that we need some supplement to complete a work. We often need the vital roles of "supporting character" (*ashirai*).

It is important to have a certain purpose when selecting the material flower as a third "supporting character" and after. Do not select the material flowers only because you like them. Your precious work will be compromised, becoming just an "Assortment of my favorite flowers."

作品 68　ゆり　かすみ草　ポトス　バラ
Work 68　Materials: Lily, Gypsophila, Pothos, Rose

ピンクのゆりを白い小花のかすみ草と取り合わせ、少女のような雰囲気をイメージしています。舞台となる花器も明るい黄色で楽しげな形をしたものを選びました。空間を引き締めるポトスとアクセントとしてのバラが作品を仕上げる脇役となっています。

The pink lily and gypsophila create the image of a little girl. The vase, the stage for the girl, is bright yellow and its shape is smiling happily. Supporting characters to complete the work are the leaves of pothos scattered around within the space and a rose highlighting the whole image as an accent.

作品 69 ゆり 山しだ カラテア バラ
Work 69　Materials: Lily, Dicranopteris linearis (fern), Calathea, Rose

作品 68 と同じゆりに黒く着色した山しだを出合わせ、大人の女性の雰囲気にしました。器も落ち着いた色のものを使用し、葉も暗色のカラテアを用いています。同じゆりでも、取り合わせる花材によって雰囲気が全く異なるという一例です。逆にいえば、表現に応じて花材を取り合わせることが大切だということです。

The lily used in work 68, the fern is painted black, and the girl has grown up to be a lady. The vase used for this work is dark-colored, and so are the leaves of calathea. It is an example showing that the same lily can change the atmosphere depending on other material flowers chosen to sit with it. In other words, it is important to select flowers to arrange together depending on the desired expression.

表現に基づく構成、手法の多様性

　表現について、一般的には「自然的表現」と「非自然的表現」に分類されます。では、一般的にいう「自然的表現」「非自然的表現」とは、どのようなことをいうのでしょうか。順に考察してみましょう。

　「自然的表現」とは、自然界のありさまなどと関連した表現を意味し、季節感、景観美、出生美などを捉えた表現といえます。一方で、「非自然的表現」とは、自然界とは直接に関連しない表現、例えば、個々の花材が持つ色、形、質から作者自身が感じ取ったイメージをいけ表わすような場合を意味し、「心象の花」とも呼ばれます。

　また、表現の分類とは別に、構成や手法においても「自然的」と「非自然的」に分類することができます。「自然的構成」や「自然的手法」とは、植物が自然界で生育しているような用い方、つまり向日性などを考慮したようなものであるといえます。立花や生花で枝葉などを省略して幹の動きを生かすことや、風に吹かれた茎を折れ曲がったように変形させることがありますが、自由花においても、この程度の省略や変形は「自然的手法」となります。

　そして、「非自然的構成」や「非自然的手法」とは自然界にはないような用い方であり、例えばモンステラの葉の意匠性を生かすために向日性とは関係なく面的に用いたり、表現に応じてもともとの形とまったく異なるよう変形して用いたりする場合を意味します。

Diversity in Structures and Methods Dependent on Expression

Expressions are generally classified into "naturalistic expressions" and "non-naturalistic expressions." Here, what does the "non-naturalistic expressions" mean in general terms? Now we will examine this issue.

"Naturalistic expression" is the expression related to the state of nature, and it is the expression capturing the sense of the seasons, the beauty of a landscape, and *shussho* (inner beauty of a plant) and so on. "Non-naturalistic expressions," on the other hand, is an expression not directly related to Nature, for example, an expression in which the creator uses the plants based on his/her imagined perspective, influenced perhaps by its color, shape, and texture. It's also known as "Flowers in imagination." Besides, not only the expression but also the structures and methods can be classified into "naturalistic" and "non-naturalistic." When using a "naturalistic structure" or "naturalistic method," plants are arranged as they are found naturally occurring, which means that we have to consider the natural aspects of plant growth such as the tendency of a plant to grow toward its light source (heliotropism). When arranging *rikka* or *shoka*, we often take some branches or leaves off to emphasize the movement of the stem or reshape the stem to make it look as if it is bended in the wind. In *jiyuka*, also, these kinds of curtailments and reshaping are included in "naturalistic methods." When using a "non-naturalistic structure" or "non-naturalistic method," plants are arranged in ways that don't occur in nature. Plants can be transformed into shapes that are different from their original shape in the nature, depending on the required expression. For example, a leaf of Monstera can be placed flatly, regardless of its heliotropism, to emphasize its shape according to the intended design of the work.

作品70 梅 椿 葉ぼたん
Work 70　Materials: Japanese plum, Camellia, Flowering cabbage

① 自然的構成や手法による自然的表現

梅の枝を花器と組み合わせ、作った空間に1輪の椿を配して春への思いを表現しています。ずわえの直線的な枝ぶりを際立たせるため、曲線を持つ器を用いました。葉ぼたんが空間を引き締める脇役です。

1) Naturalistic expression using naturalistic structure or naturalistic methods

A branch of Japanese plum is placed next to a vase. A single camellia is put in the space made by the branches, and it expresses the expectation for the coming spring. A curved round-shaped vase is used to emphasize the straightness of the plum branch. Flowering cabbage is the supporting character of this work which is scattered around the space.

作品 71　ひまわり　ダリア　アジアンタム　キーウィづる　レクス・ベゴニア　ゴールデンスティック
Work 71　Materials: Sunflower, Dahlia, Maidenhair fern, Kiwi vine, Begonia, Craspedia globosa (Golden sticks)

② 非自然的構成や手法による自然的表現

茶色のキーウィづるを組み合わせた秋色の器の中心に、夏を代表するひまわりとダリアを用い、晩夏から初秋に向かう季の移りを表しました。器との一体感を求めて、ひまわりと同系色の小さなゴールデンスティックを花瓶口より下の空間に用いました。

2) Naturalistic expression using non-naturalistic structure or non-naturalistic methods

Sunflower and dahlia, which represent summer, are positioned in the center of the autumn-color vase decorated with kiwi vine. The image of the work is the transition of the seasons from late summer to early fall. Small golden sticks, which has similar color to sunflower, are placed in the space under the vase opening, to make the whole work take on a sense of oneness.

作品 72　カラー　アンスリウム　グリーントリフ　バラ　ブルースター
Work 72　Materials: Calla, Anthurium, Dianthus, Rose, Iweedia caerulea

③ 自然的構成や手法による非自然的表現

『花王以来の花伝書』に「人待花」という恋心を表現した作品があります。自然の草木の表情や動きに思いを託したロマンチックな作品です。カラーの茎の自然な曲がりを生かして、「首を長〜くして待っています！」と待ち焦がれる心を表現しました。

3) Non-naturalistic expression using naturalistic structure or naturalistic methods

A work named "Hito o matsu hana (a flower waiting for someone)" is introduced in "*Kao Irai no Kadensho*". It's a romantic work, in which the exciting feeling of love is expressed by the look and movement of the plants. The natural curve of calla is a person who is craning her neck to see if her beloved is arriving soon.

作品 73　モンステラ　アナナス　ストレリチア　ミラ
Work 73　Materials: Monstera, Ananas, Strelitzia, Milla biflora

④ 非自然的構成や手法による非自然的表現

恐竜の卵のような器に出合いました。そこから発想した「誕生」をテーマとした作品です。緑のモンステラの葉を割って出てきたような真っ赤なアナナスを中心に用い、ミラの蕾をあしらって新しい命の息吹を表しました。

4) Non-naturalistic expression using non-naturalistic structure or non-naturalistic methods

The theme of this work is "Birth." The idea was drawn from the dinosaur-egg shaped vase. The bright red ananas in the center looks as if it is emerging and tearing up the green monstera leaf. The buds of the milla biflora added to convey the image of the birth of a new life.

表現と構成の変化

●「たて」「ななめ」「よこ」について

　花材美の生かし方や表現に基づく構成として「たて」「ななめ」「よこ」の分類があります。ここで大切なことは、「たて」「ななめ」「よこ」にまとめることを制作の最初の目的としないということです。主役とする花材の生かし方を考えた上での選択であり、表現に基づく選択でなければなりません。それは、立花において直立性の若松を主役とする時に、直真（すぐしん）という「たての構成」を選択し、枝に多様な曲がりのある老松を主役とする時に、砂之物という「よこの構成」を選択するのと同様です。さらに、表現に応じて挿し口を考えることも有効です。

● 挿し口

　挿し口を一カ所にまとめることで、より強い動感を得ることができます。一方で、挿し口を分割すると、ゆったりとした雰囲気を演出できます。さらに、挿し口を前後に分割すれば、ゆったり感に加えて立体感も高まります。表現に応じて最適な挿し口を選択しましょう。

Expression Depending on Structure
● "vertical," "slanting," and "horizontal."

In the book "Ikenobo Ikebana An Introductory Free Style Curriculum," structures to enhance the impression of material flowers and structures depending on the desired expression are classified as "vertical," "slanting," and "horizontal." However, you must not set these classifications as the goal of your arrangement. You have to select "vertical," "slanting," or "horizontal" considering how you can enhance the aesthetic of the main material flowers and how you want to reveal the desired expression. For example, working on *rikka*, a "vertical structure" called *sugushin* is chosen when using an erect young pine tree as the main material, and a "horizontal structure" such as *sunanomono* is chosen when using old pine tree with gnarled branches.

Besides the structure of orientation, different types of *sashikuhi* can be effective according to the expression desired.

● *Sashikuchi* (Positioning)

Sashikuchi is the positions of the cut stems of material flowers placed in the vessel. Positioning the flowers together in one place gives dynamism to the work, while dividing or separating the materials conveys spaciousness. Dividing the materials to the back and front adds a sense of depth. You can try to select the most appropriate *sashikuchi* for the materials on hand, depending on what you want to express.

作品 74 ききょう 矢筈すすき おみなえし ヒペリクム レクス・ベゴニア
Work 74 Materials: Japanese bellflower, Eulalia, Patrinia scabiosifolia, Hypericum, Begonia

秋風に吹かれるききょうの姿を矢筈すすきが作る空間で表現しました。挿し口を一カ所にまとめることで、ききょうの動感を強調しています。

Japanese bellflowers blown in the autumn wind are expressed in the space created using eulalia. Positioning the cut stems of all materials at one place (i.e. having one *sashikuchi*) emphasize the dynamism of Japanese bellflowers.

作品 75 ききょう　矢筈すすき　おみなえし　ヒペリクム　レクス・ベゴニア
Work 75 Materials: Japanese bellflower, Eulalia, Patrinia scabiosifolia, Hypericum, Begonia

作品74と同じ取り合わせで挿し口を分割したものです。両方の作品を比較してみると、挿し口を分割することで、ききょうが秋風に吹かれてゆらゆらと揺れる雰囲気をより強調しています。両者のどちらがより良いということではなく、求める雰囲気に応じて挿し口についても考える必要があるということです。

Same materials as in work 74, but the *sashikuchi* is separated this time. When comparing the two works, flowers of Japanese bellflower, which are positioned separately, look more like they are swaying softly in the autumn breeze. The point is not which of them is better, but that we have to consider the positioning of materials is governed by the atmosphere we want to create.

● 連瓶

挿し口の分割の発展形として、複数の花器を用いた分割が考えられます。この方法の利点は、複数の花器の置き方によってさまざまな空間を作り出せるということです。草木の表情や枝ぶりの生かし方、求める表現に応じていろいろ試してください。

また、飾る環境などに応じて花器の数を調整し、作品のサイズを変えることも可能です。この場合、それぞれの花器に配する花材などの関連性によって一体感を持たせることが大切です。

● Renpei (Using several vases for one work)

Developed from the method to separate materials into two or more different positions, it is possible to use several vases for one work. The merit of this method is that it can suggest various images depending on how each vase is placed. You can try as many styles you want to express, by considering how you use the expression that each plant has or the shape of branches.

You can also change the number of vases to use and the size of the work depending on the display environment. In this case, it is important to bring together the whole work by considering, for example, what material flowers you should put in each vase.

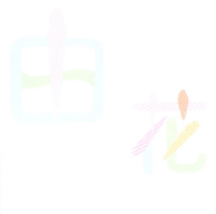

作品 76　木いちご　秋明菊　糸菊　小菊
Work 76　Materials: Raspberry, Japanese anemone, Chrysanthemum, Small chrysanthemum

連瓶の場合、花器の並べ方によって空間の広がりや立体感など、表現に基づくさまざまな雰囲気を演出することができるのが特徴です。作品は、紅葉した木いちごの葉を背景に、秋を代表する菊の彩りを生かしました。器を左右に配置した場合と、前後に配置した場合を比較してみてください。

When using several vases for one work, you can create a variety of atmospheres, such as an expanse of space or a sense of depth, by changing the layout of the vases. In this work, colors of chrysanthemum, which represent autumn, are used in the center, with the autumn-colored leaves of raspberry as background. Please compare the two versions, one with the vases placed side by side and the other with the vases placed behind and in front of each other.

作品 77　アンスリウム　アスパラガス　バンダ　ポトス
Work 77　Materials: Anthurium, Asparagus, Vanda orchid, Pothos

つった透明のガラス器に南国の花を取り合わせました。アスパラガスの軽やかな動きで涼感を演出し、さらに連瓶とすることで「南国の休日」の穏やかさをも表現しました。

A variety of tropical flowers are put together in suspended-type clear glass vases. Airy movement of asparagus provides a cool feeling, as well as a relaxing "tropical holiday" is expressed by using two vases.

作品 78 シクラメン
Work 78 Materials: Cyclamen

紹興酒を飲む小さなグラスにシクラメンの表情を捉えて連瓶とした作品です。テーマは「チームIKENOBO」。実は、花の仲間たちに器と花を渡し、一人一人にそれぞれ花の表情を生かして制作してもらいました。それらを私が空間美を考慮しながら並べたもので、花の自然美を生かした癒やし系の自由花です。花留には事務用クリップを用いています。

The theme of this work is "team Ikenobo." Shaoxing rice wine glasses, each of which has a cyclamen showing different aspects, standing in line. In fact, I gave a glass and a cyclamen to my ikebana colleagues, and each of them worked on capturing its best aspect and positioning in its glass. Then, I set them in a line, considering the beauty of space, so the natural beauty of the flowers provides therapeutic atmosphere. Paper clips are used to hold the flowers in the glasses.

制作プロセスのおさらい

ドラマを作り出すおさらいとして、制作のプロセスを分解写真で解説してみましょう。

● 花材からの発想

Motif, or Idea → Expression → Materials → Structures → Methods

As a review of a way to make dramas, these photographs show you the process of arrangement.

- **Motif from floral materials**

①「難を転ずる」といわれる南天を放射状に構成します。「新年の安泰」を祈念したお正月の花です。

② 赤い南天の実との対照効果を求めて明るいピンクのランを取り合わせ、シクラメンで花器口を引き締めました。

③ 南天の動きに合わせて背景に金の水引を扇形に配し、末広がりの発展性を演出しています。

1) This is an ikebana for the New Year which wishes for the "peace of the new year," with nandina arranged in a radial fashion. The name nandina is said to mean "to turn difficulty into happiness."
2) Bright pink orchid is added for contrast against red nandina berries. Cyclamen accentuates the mouth of the vase.
3) Golden *mizuhiki* (paper string used to tie presents) is arranged in a radial fashion to fit with the movement of nandina, and it creates an image of everlasting development.

作品 79　南天　ラン　シクラメン
Work 79　Materials: Nandina, Orchid, Cyclamen

● 器からの発想

●Motif Idea from the vase

①澄み切った秋空のような色合いの器から発想し、その秋空に咲き誇るように秋明菊を配しました。

②交差するようにゆったりといけたミスカンツスで、爽やかな秋風を感じさせます。

③白い秋明菊を際立たせるように、濃い色合いのヒューケラとりんどうで花器口を引き締めて完成です。

1) Getting an idea from the vase whose color is that of a clear autumn sky, Japanese anemone are arranged as if they bloom in the sky.
2) Miscanthus, which cross over each other in relaxing way, creates the image of a pleasant autumn breeze.
3) Dark-colored heuchera and gentian placed at the mouths of the vase emphasize the white color of the Japanese anemone.

作品80　秋明菊　ミスカンツス　ヒューケラ　りんどう
Work 80　Materials: Japanese anemone, Miscanthus, Heuchera, Gentian

● 環境からの発想

●Motif from environment

①入学式の受付に飾る花です。歓迎ムードを表現するためにスイートピーを開放的に構成します。

②中心を華やかな草花で引き締め、スイートピーの動きと対照させます。

③柔らかなゼラニウムの緑葉を加えて仕上げます。

1) This is an ikebana to display at a school entrance ceremony. Sweet pea is placed expansively to create welcoming atmosphere.
2) Center of the work is located with the bright flowers, so they contrast with the movement of sweet pea.
3) Soft green leaves of geranium are added to complete the work.

作品 81
アネモネ　スイートピー
ラッパ水仙　ゼラニウム
Work 81　Materials: Anemone, Sweet pea, Daffodil, Geranium

● 行事からの発想

●Motif from event

①父の日に贈るレリーフです。写真を中心にワインボトルとグラスで土台を構成します。

②ボトルとグラスに水を入れて花材をいけます。黒いワイヤーに巻き付けるようにアイビーを構成し、ワイナリーの雰囲気を演出します。

③父の日の花であるバラをいけて、娘からのハッピー・ファーザーズ・デイ！

1) This is a relief for Father's Day. Base is made with a wine bottle and a glass, with a photo in the center.
2) Material flowers is placed in the bottle and the glass filled with water. Ivy is looped around the black wire, so it creates a representation of a winery.
3) Rose, a flower of Father's Day, is added to complete the work. A Happy Father's Day wish from a daughter.

作品82　バラ　アイビー
Work 82　Materials: Rose, Ivy

表現と構成の多様性

いけばなの構成は、「置き」「掛け」「釣り」の三つに分類できますが、表現に基づいて構成を考えていくと、置きと掛けや、掛けと釣りのような融合的な構成が有効な場合もあります。

● 置きと釣り

Diversity in Expression and Structure

The structure of ikebana can be classified into three categories; standing-type, hanging-type, and suspended-type. However, when planning the structure, it is sometimes effective to fuse two different types, such as standing-type and hanging-type, or hanging-type and suspended-type.

• Standing-type and suspended-type

作品83　てっせん　スチールグラス
Work 83　Materials: Clematis, Xanthorrhoea

テーマ：「風と共に去り、風と共に来たる」

池坊中央研修学院祭は、一年間のまとめとしての研修発表の場ですが、共に学んだ仲間たちとの別れの時でもあります。風は常に動くものであり、人生も多くの出会いと別れの繰り返しです。「また会いましょう！」という思いを風に揺れるようになびくてっせんに託しました。

- Theme: "Gone with the wind, and come with the wind"

The Ikenobo Central Training Institute Fair is a workshop where students present their work as a summary of the year, but it is also a time for them to say good-bye to their fellow students. Life is a repetition of encounters and good-byes, just like wind blowing endlessly. A desire of meeting them again is expressed by the clematis, which sways as if waving in the wind.

置きと掛け

Standing-type and hanging-type

作品 84　桜　バラ　苔
Work 84　Materials: Prunus (cherry), Rose, Moss

テーマ：「君と出会い、君と歩く」

桜は花を咲かせて散っていきます。しかし季節は巡り、また春がやって来るのです。卒業生も在校生も、すべての仲間たちのご縁がずっと続くことを願って、しだれ桜の空間に四季咲きのバラ（コクテール）と、永遠を感じる緑の苔を取り合わせました。

・Theme: "Meeting, and living together"
Cherry blossoms bloom and then fall. However, the seasons rotate, and spring comes again. The perpetual rose named "Rose Cocktail" and green moss which makes us feel eternity are arranged in between weeping cherry trees, with the hope for eternal friendship with all fellow members, including both graduate and current students.

● 釣りと掛け

•Suspended-type and hanging-type

作品 85　松　ゆり　オンシディウム　バラ
Work 85　Materials: Pine, Lily, Oncidium orchid, Rose

テーマ:「夢一夜」
奏でる笛の音が、風に揺れる御簾の向こうから聞こえてくるような情景をイメージした作品です。壁面から松の枝を伸ばし、その空間に笛のような形の器をつりました。その字から「百人との出合い」を連想させるゆりと、華やかなランと共にみやびな光源氏の世界を表現しています。

• Theme: "One Night Dream"
This work shows the image of a scene where the sound of a Japanese flute floats out from behind *misu*, the bamboo blind, waving in the wind. A vase shaped like a flute is suspended in the space of a pine branch, which is stretching out from the wall. Lily, whose Japanese name in Chinese characters said to mean "Meeting one hundred people," and a bright oncidium orchid creates the elegant world of Hikaru Genji.

第四章 花と暮らそう！

暮らしのいけばな

生活文化としてのいけばなと発展：飾る環境との調和

　いけばなは、日本の生活文化として人々の暮らしの中で生まれ、生活様式の変遷に適応しながら発展してきました。暮らしのＴＰＯ（季と場所と行事）の中で花とのふれあいを楽しみながら花を通した人と人とのふれあいが、今日までいけばなを育んできた最も大きな要素だといえます。

● 初期の暮らしの花（『花王以来の花伝書』）と池坊いけばなの成立（『池坊専応口伝』）

　最古の花伝書といわれる『花王以来の花伝書』には、仏前供花から発展した三具足に対する記述や絵図は掲載されておらず、四季を楽しむ花、飾る環境に適応した花、さまざまな行事の花などのいけ方が記されています。つまり、最古の花伝書は、草木に思いを重ね、暮らしの中で楽しむための教えを記したものであると考えます。

　そして、京の都が焼け野原と化した応仁の乱の後、池坊専応によって池坊いけばなの原典ともいえる『池坊専応口伝』が記されます。専応の教えによって、暮らしに飾るさまざまな花に池坊いけばなとしての思想が込められ、伝統的美感と構造が備わったのです。

Chapter 4 Living with Flowers
Ikebana in Daily Life
Ikebana as a Culture for Everyday Life and Its Development: Harmony with the lifestyle

Ikebana was created as a culture bound up in people's daily lives, and has been developed adapting to the transition of lifestyle. People have enjoyed interacting with flowers in the TPO (Time which means seasons here, Place, and Occasions) in their daily life. I believe that the interaction of people through flowers is the greatest factor of the development of ikebana.

●**Preliminary daily flowers ("*Kao Irai no Kadensho*") and the establishment of Ikenobo Ikebana ("*Ikenobo Senno Kuden*")**

In the book entitled "*Kao Irai no Kadensho*," which is said to be the oldest *Kadensho*, there are no descriptions nor images for *mitsugusoku*, the term for the three implements for worship (incense burner, flower arrangement and candle-stand), which developed from flower offerings for the deceased in Buddhism.
Introduced in the *Kadensho* are the methods of display of the flowers for enjoyment of the seasons, flowers fitting for a location, and flowers at various events. In other words, the oldest *Kadensho* shows us how to focus our thoughts on plants and how to enjoy our lives.
Then, after the *Onin* war, a result of which Kyoto was largely destroyed by fire, Senno Ikenobo wrote the book

"*Ikenobo Senno Kuden*," the bible of Ikenobo Ikebana. Thanks to the teachings of Senno, spirituality as Ikenobo Ikebana has become established from the various flower displays that we encounter in our daily lives, and so also did traditional beauty and structures.

吹分花（自然の花）
Fukiwake no hana (flowers in nature)

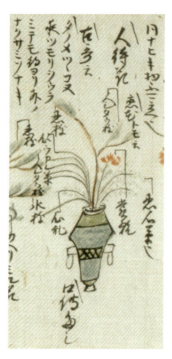
人待花（心象の花）
Hito wo matsu hana (flowers in one's mind)

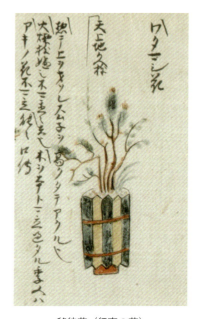
移徒花（行事の花）
Watamashi hana (flowers for events)

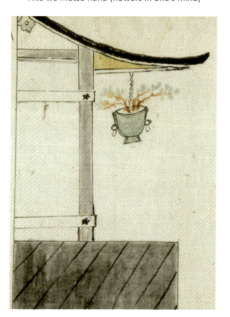
軒下花（環境の花）
Nokishita no hana (flowers in environment)

いけばな草創期（室町時代）の様子：『花王以来の花伝書』からの絵図
Beginning of ikebana (Muromachi period): image from "*Kao Irai no Kadensho*."

● いけばなは時代とともに

　室町時代に精神性が確立された池坊いけばなは、時代の変遷に適応した花型を作り出しながら今日まで発展してきました。歴史的には、立花、生花、自由花の順にととのえられていきますが、その理由は、各時代におけるいけばなを楽しむ人々の生活環境に起因しています。

　前述のように、いけばなが生まれた当初は、立花、生花、自由花といった様式の分類ではなく、表現や飾る環境による分類がなされていました。つまり、立花や生花だけが池坊の伝統ある様式ではないということです。『花王以来の花伝書』に記された机花は、急須を花器として活用しています。そして、そのいけ方は、まさに現代における自由花と同様だったのです。さらに、現代社会においては、室町時代と同様に、多様な環境に適応できる自由花の重要性が再び高まっています。

● Ikebana, with the Changing Times

Ikenobo Ikebana, which was established in the Muromachi Period, has developed until now, creating a floral model according to the changing times. These include the styles of *rikka*, *shoka*, and *jiyuka* have developed chronologically, and the order has roots in the living environment of the people who enjoyed ikebana in each period. As I have explained above, when ikebana began, it was not categorized by styles such as *rikka*, *shoka*, and *jiyuka*, but by the message of the work or environment in which it was to be displayed. In other words, it is not only *rikka* and *shoka* that is a traditional style of Ikenobo. "*Tsukue bana* (flowers on the desk)" in the book "*Kao Irai no Kadensho*" utilizes a teapot as a vase and the method employed for the arrangement is just the same as for current *jiyuka*. Besides, the importance of *jiyuka*, which can be adjusted to a diversity of environments, has increased in modern society again just as in the Muromachi Period.

二代専好立花図（御所）
Senko II Rikka-zu (Kyoto Imperial Palace)

上流階級のいけばな（戦国時代〜江戸初期）：
大砂物（神内曙光）
Ikebana for the upper-class (Sengoku period to early Edo period):
O-sunamono (Prof. Kouchi Shokou)

一般庶民も楽しむ床の間のいけばな（江戸中期〜）：女性が生花を楽しむ絵図　　　『千代田の大奥』国立国会図書館
Ikebana for *tokonoma*, which ordinary people also enjoyed (since the mid Edo period): Image of women enjoying *Shoka*.

多様な生活空間に飾る現代のいけばな
Modern ikebana to display in various living spaces

現代生活に飾る花

「花は、心のビタミンＣ！」と、若い頃に習ったことがありました。現代社会は、科学技術の進歩によってどんどん便利になる反面、無機質な空間でふれあい不足になりがちです。こんな時代だからこそ、命ある花とのふれあいを楽しみ、癒やしの花を暮らしに飾りましょう。

● 飾る環境と表現に応じた構成と手法

『花王以来の花伝書』にも記されているように、環境に応じた花の飾り方やいけ方を大別すると、「置き」「掛け」「釣り」の三つに分類することができます。飾る環境や表現に応じて、三つのいけ方の中から適切なものを選択するわけです。また、前述のように表現や花材美に基づいて「たて」「ななめ」「よこ」の構成も選択します。さらに、表現を高めるための手法も工夫しましょう。

Contemporary Flower Displays

When I was young, I was taught "Flowers are vitamin C for the mind." While modern life is becoming more and more convenient with technical progress, we tend to lack interaction with others in an inorganic space. Now is the time we should enjoy interaction with living flowers and display them to decorative effect in our lives.

● Structure and Style Appropriate to the Message of the Work and Environment to Display

As it is written in *"Kao Irai no Kadensho,"* methods of display and style of arrangements are classified roughly into three categories, based on the environment where they are displayed. The three categories are standing-type, hanging-type, and suspended-type. We choose the one appropriate to the environment to display or message of the work among the three styles. Also, as I mentioned above, we choose structures such as vertical, slanting, and horizontal, based on the message of the work and the aesthetics of the material flowers. We need to be creative with the method to enhance our expression.

玄関 Entrance

作品 86 ポピー　雪柳　パンジー　グリーントリフ　鳴子ゆり
Work 86 Materials: Poppy, Spiraea thunbergii, Pansy, Dianthus, Solomon's seal

玄関に春の装いを添える自由花。器の窓から明るい彩りのポピーが飛び出して、春の到来を告げるかのようです。花器の上口には、かわいいパンジーをリズミカルに並列させて春の喜びを表現しました。

Jiyuka to add a taste of spring to an entrance. A colorful poppy jumps out from the window of the vase, as if heralding the arrival of spring. The charming pansies arranged rhythmically on the top of the vase represent the joy of spring.

作品 87 アンスリウム　玉しだ　桜小町（シレネ）　ゴールデンスティック
Work 87 Materials: Anthurium, Sword fern, Silene, Craspedia globosa (Golden sticks)

アンスリウムのかわいらしい表情に「春が来た！」という思いを託しました。黄緑色の柔らかな玉しだが季節感を演出し、春らしい桜小町（シレネ）とゴールデンスティックで足元を引き締めています。

The endearing impression of anthurium expresses the feeling that "spring has come." The yellow-green, soft sword ferns create a feeling of the season too, and spring-like silene and golden sticks brighten the bottom.

作品 88　ななかまど　ききょう　けいとう　さんきらい
Work 88　Materials: Mountain ash, Japanese bellflower, Common cockscomb, Greenbrier

ひなびた味わいの籠にいけた、秋を楽しむ玄関の花です。これから色づいていくさんきらいの実を溢れんばかりに盛り、色鮮やかな秋の草花を取り合わせました。

Jiyuka of autumn arranged in a rustic basket. The basket is filled to the brim with the berries of greenbriers, which are about to take on autumn colors, and colorful autumn flowers are arranged on top.

作品89　スイートピー　グロリオサ　オブリザツム　ライムポトス　かすみ草
Work 89　Materials: Sweet pea, Gloriosa, Obryzatum orchid, Lime Pothos, Gypsophila

華やかなスイートピーを主役として、春霞の中を蝶が舞う様子をイメージした掛け花です。ステンレスの直線が草花の柔らかさを際立たせ、掛けることで軽やかさを強調しています。玄関に絵や写真を掛ける代わりに、こんな掛け花はいかがでしょうか。

This is a hanging-type work that evokes images of butterflies floating in the spring haze, with bright sweet peas as the principal part. The straight lines of stainless highlight the tenderness of the flowers, and their lightness is emphasized by hanging it on the wall. How would you like to have such a hanging ikebana on the wall of an entrance instead of paintings or photographs?

床の間 Tokonoma

作品 90 いたやかえで　バラ　あじさい
Work 90 Materials: Maple, Rose, Hydrangea

挿し口を分割する構成で水面の清らかさを演出しています。石や剣山などを用いず、透明の塩ビ板に開けた数カ所の穴に花材を挿していけ、水をたっぷりと見せました。じめじめとした梅雨時に涼しさを求めた、床の間の花です。

Materials are separated into two different positions of the vessel so the surface of the pure water is visible. Transparent PVC board with holes is used to hold the flowers, instead of stones or *Kenzan*, and so making the water as visible as possible. This is an ikebana for a *tokonoma* which cools down the clammy rainy season.

作品 91　カトレア　オブリザツム　ベゴニア　トルコぎきょう　ミスカンツス
Work 91　Materials: Cattleya orchid, Obryzatum orchid, Begonia, Prairie gentian, Miscanthus

白木の台の上下に竹の器でいけました。下の釣り花は軽やかに、上の花はマッスで構成し、変化を持たせています。上下両方に用いたベゴニアの緑葉が作品のまとめ役です。

Arranged in a bamboo vase on and within a plain-wood table. The suspended-type work under the table is designed airy, and flowers on the table are arranged in an agglomeration to convey appreciation of diversity. The green leaves of begonia used in both arrangements provide a sense of oneness.

作品 92　パフィオペディルム　桃　菜の花　ゼラニウム
Work 92　Materials: Paphiopedilum orchid, Peach, Field mustard, Geranium

赤いフェルトで覆った土台にペアの器を取り付け、桃の枝の広がりの中に2輪のランの凛とした姿を生かしました。柔らかな菜の花とゼラニウムの緑葉で花器口をまとめています。ひな祭りを彩る床の間の花です。

A pair of flower vases is attached to a base covered with red felt. Two orchids stand dignified among outspreading peach branches, with soft rape blossoms and green leaves of geranium covering the mouths of the vases. This is the ikebana to brighten the *tokonoma* for *Hina-matsuri*, the Festival of Dolls.

リビングルーム Living room

参照 ▶ P71 作品62
Work 62: refer to page 71

作品93　カルセオラリア　レウココリネ　玉しだ
Work 93　Materials: Calceolaria, Leucocoryne, Sword fern

ヤシの実をくり抜いて食器としたものを器としました。柔らかな質感と優しい草花でお客さまをお迎えするセンターピースの花です。器の中の金色も見せるため、透明のペットボトルを細く切ったものを花留として活用しています。

The vessel is a dinner bowl which is actually a coconut shell. This is the ikebana as a centerpiece, which welcomes guests, and with it the soft texture of the tender plants within. There is a thinly cut transparent PET bottle as *hanadome* (flower support), so the gold color in the vessel is visible as well.

作品 94　アネモネ　レウココリネ　オンシディウム　レースフラワー　スマイラックス
Work 94　Materials: Anemone, Leucocoryne, Oncidium orchid, Lace flower, Asparagus 'smailax'

透明のガラス器の中に銀の花器を重ねたすてきな器です。パーティーの華やかさを演出するため、色や形や大きさの対照効果を考えながら色とりどりの草花を取り合わせました。緑のスマイラックスを透明のガラス器の中にもいけて、みずみずしさを与えるとともに一体感を求めています。

A beautiful combination of a silver vase in a bigger glass vase base. To create the image of a joyous party, flowers of many different colors are arranged together, taking into consideration the effect of the comparison of their color, shape, and size. The green asparagus 'smailax' in the outer glass vase provides a freshness to the work as well as a feeling of oneness.

作品 95　シクラメン　キーウィづる
Work 95　Materials: Cyclamen, Kiwi vine

リビングテーブルの上に飾る花です。ガラスの灰皿を器とし、キーウィづるをはめ込んで花留としました。ガラスの質感とシクラメンの花がよくマッチしていますが、2色の花の配置と葉の先の向きも重要なポイントです。

This is the ikebana to display on the table in the living room. A glass ashtray is used as a vessel, and kiwi vines are set in it to use as *hanadome* (flower support). The texture of the glass and the flowers of cyclamen matches to each other very well. However, the position of the two different colors of flowers and direction of leaf tips are also important point of this work.

参照 ▶ P69 作品 60
Work 60: refer to page 69

作品 96　ゆり　アルストロメリア　かすみ草　鳴子ゆり
Work 96　Materials: Lily, Alstroemeria, Gypsophila, Solomon's seal

信楽焼の食器にかすみ草のマッスを重ね、ふんわりとした雰囲気を作りました。そこから伸びたゆりの優しげな表情を捉えた癒やし系の作品です。花留はペットボトルの底に穴を開けたものを花器の底に固定して、そこにかすみ草とゆりをいけました。アルストロメリアと鳴子ゆりは、かすみ草のマッスに挿して留めています。

The airy image is created on the *Shigaraki-yaki* bowl by putting a mass of gypsophila in it. Gently stretching lilies give the work therapeutic atmosphere. Gypsophila and lilies are in a PET bottle with holes on the bottom, which is set in the bowl. Alstroemeria and Solomon's seal are positioned through the mass of gypsophila.

机の花 Flowers on the Desk

参照 ▶ P33
refer to page 33

作品 97　シンフォリカルポス　シクラメン　玉しだ　ブルーキャッツアイ
Work 97　Materials: Symphoricarpos, Cyclamen, Sword fern, Otacanthus caeruleus

『花王以来の花伝書』に「机花」が記されており、「筆や紙の方へ花をなびかせるな」との教えがあります。その教えに基づいた机に飾るミニチュア自由花です。下葉を省略した玉しだの軽やかな動きが構成のポイントです。

In the *"Kao Irai no Kadensho,"* *"tsukue bana"* is described as "Don't let the flowers swing to the pen and papers." This work is a miniature *jiyuka*, which follows the lesson. The point of the arrangement is sword ferns whose lower leaves are cut off to make them look springy.

作品 98　アンスリウム　レウココリネ　グリーントリフ
Work 98　Materials: Anthurium, Leucocoryne, Dianthus

家族の写真と共に飾って、お客さまをお迎えする花です。グリーントリフをカップに挿し入れて花留としました。「ようこそ！」という声が聞こえてきそうです。

This ikebana welcomes guests with a family photo. Dianthus in the cup works as a *hanadome* (flower support). It looks as if we can hear it say "Welcome."

食卓 Dining Table

作品99 南天　菜の花　レリア　ゼラニウム
Work 99　Materials: Nandina, Field mustard, Laelia orchid, Geranium

穴を開けた塩ビ板をお皿に敷いて、菜の花と南天の実を盛り付けて「花のサラダ」のようにいけました。レリアは、フォークの先に挿し込んで留めています。軽い花であればフォークの重量が支えてくれます。グッド・モーニング！今日もすてきな一日を！

Field mustard and berries of nandina are put on a PVC board with holes, placed on a dish, so it looks like a "salad of flowers." Laelia orchid is stopped by inserting it into the fork tines. The relatively heavy weight of the fork can support light flowers. "Good morning, and have a wonderful day."

木製のお皿とスプーンを用いました。スプーンの穴に草花を挿して留めています。水面の清らかさが、花たちの美しさを引き立て、ゆったりとしたランチタイムを演出します。

A wooden plate and skimmers are used for this arrangement. Plants are inserted into the holes of the skimmers so they are held stably. The clear water surface brings out the beauty of the flowers. With this ikebana on the table, we can enjoy a leisurely lunchtime.

作品 100　ペツニア　オンシディウム
Work 100　Materials: Petunia, Oncidium orchid

食器の中に網を敷いてレタスをおいしそうに盛り付け、その網の目に花を挿しました。ハイビスカスとヤシの葉のなびきで夏の食卓を飾ります。

The lettuce on the dish looks very delicious. Flowers are placed on it, positioned through a net under the lettuce. Hibiscus and the swing of palm make the summer dining table very special.

作品 101　ハイビスカス
アレカヤシ　レタス
Work 101　Materials: Hibiscus, Palm, Lettuce

行事の花

日本人は、さまざまな行事や節目において、その思いを自然が作り出した草木の美しさに重ね、表現してきました。例えば、室町時代に記された『仙伝抄』の「移徒花（新築や転居祝いの花）」には、「一切赤きは猶嫌うなり」と記され、「火事を連想させる赤い花をいけてはいけない」という教えが記されています。このことは、単にきれいな花を飾るのではなく、草木が持つ色に人々が意味を見いだして、表現に基づく思いを託してきたことが感じられます。

ある時、海外の方から松竹梅に対する質問を受けました。「松も竹も花はないし、梅は一年の一時期しか花を咲かせない。そんな松や竹、梅を祝儀に用いるとは、日本にはきれいな花がないのか」というものでした。その問いに対して、松竹梅に人の生き方を重ね合わせて祝儀に用いられる意味を説明した思い出があります。

日本で生まれたいけばなは、単なる外見的な美しさだけではなく、個々の草木の生きてきた様子にも思いを託していることが特質であり、生きているものの美しさを捉えて表現するのが、池坊いけばなの基本です。だからこそ川端康成も『池坊専応口伝』の解釈として「枯れた枝にも『花』がある」と述べています。花に思いを託したり、意味を与えたりすることが池坊いけばなの特質なのです。

Flowers for Events

On various occasions, Japanese people have repeatedly expressed their thoughts on the beauty of plants as they occur in nature. In the book "*Sendensho*," for example, it is stated that "*watamashi hana* (flowers to celebrate relocation or housewarming) hate all red colors," which means that "we must not use red flowers because they are implicative of fire." We can learn from this that Japanese people have not only displayed beautiful flowers but found meanings in the colors of plants and associated a feeling or expression with the colors.

I was once asked a question about *Sho-chiku-bai* (pine, bamboo, and Japanese plum) by a non-Japanese person. "Pines and bamboos don't have blossoms, and Japanese plums blossom only one season in a year. Why do Japanese people use those trees for celebration? Don't you have beautiful flowers or blossoms in Japan?" It is a good memory that I explained to him that we liken our lives to *Sho-chiku-bai* and so we use them for celebration.

Ikebana, which is created in Japan, is not only the beauty of appearance, but the way to express our feelings through the lives of plants. The fundamental point of Ikenobo Ikebana is to catch and express the beauty of living things. That is why Yasunari Kawabata stated as an interpretation of "*Ikenobo Senno Kuden*" that "there is beauty even in withered branches." To place our feelings on flowers and to give meanings to them are the essence of Ikenobo Ikebana.

青竹を組み合わせて和紙を巻いた器をつくりました。新年の大空に広がるように配したうらじろのつくる空間に紅白の花を配した、お正月を祝う花です。左右に配したしらが松が作品をまとめる役割を果たしています。

This vase is made of a combination of many different shapes of green bamboo and Japanese traditional handmade paper wrapped around them. This is an ikebana to celebrate the New Year, with the gleichenia arranged as if it is spreading out into the New Year sky, and red and white flowers placed in the space created by the gleichenia. Variegated pine, which is positioned on the left and right sides of the vase, provides composure to the work.

作品 102　うらじろ
コチョウラン　バラ　しらが松
Work 102　Materials: Gleichenia, Phalaenopsis aphrodite orchid, Rose, Variegated pine

参照 ▶ P71 作品 62
Work 62: refer to page 71

だるま型のグラスを重ねて「七転び八起き」の思いを込めていけました。シクラメンの広がりで新年の発展を祈念し、せんりょうで足元を引き締めてシンプルにまとめています。蕾の表情が空間に変化を与えるポイントです。花留はペットボトルを用いています。

The spirit of "never give up" is expressed in the two *daruma*-shaped glasses stacked vertically. The spreading out cyclamen represents the hope for the New Year, and sarcandra adds an accent to the work, and simplifies the work as well. The point of this work is the buds of cyclamen which provides a change in the space. PET bottle material is used as a *hanadome* (flower support).

作品 103　シクラメン　せんりょう
Work 103　Materials:
Cyclamen, Sarcandra glabra (Sarcandra)

作品 104　グロリオサ　かすみ草　オンシディウム　ミラ　レクス・ベゴニア
Work 104　Materials: Gloriosa, Gypsophila, Oncidium orchid, Milla biflora, Begonia

黒い塩ビ板を2枚重ね、その間に花入れを施しています。前の板に三角形の窓を開け、その周りに金色のテープでクリスマスツリーの模様を描きました。ホワイトクリスマスに降り積もる雪をかすみ草で表現し、クリスマスツリーの飾り付けをイメージしながら花を配しています。

A water jug is placed between the two layers of black PVC board. A triangle-shaped opening has been cut off from the front board, and a Christmas tree was drawn around it with golden-color tape. Gypsophila represents snowfall piling up for a white Christmas. The colors of the flowers are also positioned with the image of Christmas tree decoration.

作品 105　ポインセチア　ひいらぎ　オブリザツム　水仙
Work 105　Materials: Poinsettia, Holly, Obryzatum orchid, Narcissus

細長いガラス器にクリスマスキャンドルをイメージしていけました。ポインセチアを中心にオブリザツムで光の広がりを感じさせています。クリスマスのアクセントとして星の形をした1輪の水仙を添えました。

This work is arranged in a long and thin glass vase, so one might imagine a Christmas candle. It has a poinsettia at the center, and the obryzatum orchid flower around it represents the diffusion halo of light. A star-shaped narcissus is added as a Christmas accent.

> **その他の行事の花：**
> Other Flowers for events
>
> 作品11（P23）、作品29（P42）、
> 作品79（P94）、作品82（P97）、
> 作品92（P112）
>
> Work 11 (page 23), Work 29 (page 42),
> Work 79 (page 94), Work 82 (page 97),
> Work 92 (page 112)

おわりに

　時代とともに歩み続け、本年、歴史にその名を刻まれて555年目を迎えた池坊。それは、代々の家元が時代に適応するいけばなを生み出し、発展させてこられた歩みそのものだと思います。「門弟は今日の花をいける。家元は明日の花をいける」という言葉を聞いたことがありますが、池坊の歴代家元は、まさにそのように歩んでこられたのです。

　専永家元も「新風体」という時代の花を生み出されました。そして、その背景には、「形から姿へ」という時代に適応したお考えがあり、また「いけるということ」に対する原点回帰への指針であると認識しています。本書もそのような考えで執筆させていただきました。「自由花は、つくる」という時代は終わり、これからは「自由花も、いける」という時代になっていくであろうと思います。

　池坊専慶の活躍が歴史に刻まれた寛正3年（1462）。専慶の花の世界は、どのようなものだったのか……。専慶の花の本意は、いけばな発祥の地である六角堂の至る所にいけられた四季折々の「おもてなしの花」にあったのではないでしょうか。境内のあちこちに、置いたり、掛けたり、つったり、六角堂にお参りに来る人々をもてなす花が、専慶の世界にあったような気がしてなりません。仏前供花から発展した立て花も立てたのでしょうが、それ以上に暮らしに飾るさまざまな花をいけておられたのではないかと想像します。そして、その様子が『花王以来の花伝書』に記された作品群につながっているように思えるのです。

　池坊いけばなは、日本の伝統文化の中でも生活に根差した文化として発展してきました。専好次期家元は、「初代専好というと、私たち池坊人は、前田邸の大砂物を思い浮かべます。しかし、専好の花の世界は、大砂物だけではないはずです。彼は、戦国時代という時代における"現代の花"をいけていたはずです。そして、代々の池坊人がおのおのの生きた時代に適応した"現代の花"をいけ続けてきたことによって、今日まで池坊の花が続いてきたのだと思います。つまり、池坊いけばなは、"時代の現代文化"なのです」と、述べられています。まさに池坊いけばなの特質を知る言葉です。私も、この"時代の現代文化"という言葉を胸に、今後とも精進してまいりたいと思います。

　最後になりましたが、本書の執筆にあたっては、池坊専永家元、池坊専好次期家元、池坊雅史事務総長はじめ数多くの方々にお力添えを賜りました。拙作の写真を撮影いただいた木村尚達様、さまざまな花材をご準備いただいた花市商店の皆さま、そしていつも応援してくれる花の仲間たち。すべての皆さまに、心より厚く御礼申し上げます。

野田　学

And last but not least...

This year it is 555 years since Ikenobo made its historical mark, and all the time moving with the times. I believe it is because of the effort of successive headmasters who have created and developed ikebana to adapt to the changing times. I have heard the statement that "disciples arrange flowers for today, and the headmaster arranges flowers for tomorrow," and that is exactly how successive headmasters of Ikenobo have lived their lives. Current headmaster Sen'ei Ikenobo also produced a new style, "*shimputai*," for the contemporary world. I believe that he had ideas which adapted to the age of "From shape to style" behind the production of this new style and also that it was an idea to return to our original concept, "to revive the flowers." I wrote this book based on such ideas. I believe that the age of "designing *jiyuka*" will be over and that the age of "reviving *jiyuka*" will come.

In the year 1462, the success of Senkei Ikenobo was recorded in history. I wonder what the world of flowers of Senkei was like.

I believe his intentions were apparent in the "flowers of hospitality" of each season displayed everywhere around Rokkakudo Temple, the birthplace of ikebana. I can easily imagine that the world of Senkei had a lot of flowers standing, being suspended, and draped all around in the temple grounds to welcome and entertain the people who visited Rokkakudo Temple. I am sure he arranged *tatehana* developed from floral offerings at a Buddhist alter as well, but I also believe he arranged more ikebana to display in daily life. The series of work described in "*Kao Irai no Kadensho*" must include many of these flowers.

Among traditional cultures in Japan, Ikenobo Ikebana has developed as culture for everyday life. Headmaster Designate Senko Ikenobo says, "When talking about Senko I, we, Ikenobo people, think of *o-sunanomomo* at Maeda Residence. But the world of flowers of Senko is not just *o-sunanomomo*. I'm sure he was arranging "contemporary flowers" in the Sengoku period. And, it is because of generations of Ikenobo people who continued with the work of arranging the "contemporary flowers" of their own time that flowers of Ikenobo have continued until today. In other words, Ikenobo Ikebana is a "contemporary culture of every period." This precisely explains the characteristics of Ikenobo Ikebana. I am going continue making further efforts in my work, keeping her words, "contemporary culture of every period," in my mind.

In the end, I received a lot of support from a substantial number of people in writing this book, including Headmaster Sen'ei Ikenobo, Headmaster Designate Senko Ikenobo, Secretary-General Masafumi Ikenobo. Mr. Naotatsu Kimura who took photographs of my work, the staff of Hanaichi Shoten who prepared various flowers, and Ikenobo friends who always support me. I would like to express my deepest gratitude to all of you.

Manabu Noda

作品 106 　アルストロメリア　チューリップ　アジアンタム
Work 106 　Materials: Alstroemeria, Tulip, Maidenhair fern

　本書最後の作品は、皆さんとの乾杯の花です。アルミ板を曲げた土台にグラスを取り付けました。明るい色合いの花々とみずみずしい緑の広がりで皆さんのご多幸とご発展を祈念しています。池坊伝統の心を現代へ、そして未来へ！皆で花とのふれあいを楽しみましょう。乾杯！！

The last piece of work in this book is for a toast with you. Two glasses are attached to a bent aluminum sheet base. The colorful flowers and fresh green spreading out around them are wishing you all the best. Let's bring forward the traditional spirit of Ikenobo to the present day, and to the future. Let's enjoy our interaction with the world of flowers together. Cheers.

野田 学(のだ まなぶ)

1958年　10月4日、兵庫県尼崎市に生まれる
1978年　池坊入門
1984年　米国イリノイ大学 アジア研究科 修士課程卒業
2010年　池坊中央研修学院教授

自由花がもっと楽しくなる本
JOY OF IKENOBO FREE STYLE

2017年11月9日　第1版第1刷発行
2021年7月15日　　　　　第2刷発行

監　修　池坊専永
著　者　野田 学
発行者　池坊雅史
発行所　株式会社日本華道社
　　　　〒604-8134 京都市中京区烏丸三条下ル 池坊内
　　　　Tel 075-223-0613
編　集　日本華道社編集部
撮　影　木村尚達 ほか
デザイン　Seeds of Communication
翻　訳　株式会社 京あはせ
印刷・製本　図書印刷株式会社

©Manabu Noda 2017 Printed in Japan
ISBN978-4-89088-128-4
定価はカバーに表示してあります。

乱丁・落丁本はお取替えいたします。
本書のコピー、スキャン、デジタル化等の無断複製を禁じます。